— LOST LINES —
LONDON
NIGEL WELBOURN

Ian Allan
PUBLISHING

CONTENTS

First published 1998
Reprinted 1999, 2000 ,2001 and 2003
This impression 2004

ISBN 0 7110 2623 8

Published by Ian Allan Publishing

an imprint of Ian Allan Publishing Ltd, Hersham, Surrey KT12 4RG.
Printed in England by Ian Allan Printing Ltd, Hersham, Surrey KT12 4RG.

Code: 0411/A

ACKNOWLEDGEMENTS

I would like to thank all those who helped me with this book.
In particular, I would like to thank my parents whose patience and understanding when I was younger
allowed me to visit so many lines that are now closed.
I would also like to thank R. Trill. P. Deehan, B. O'Keeffe, M. Pocock and my father
for their assistance with this book.

Cover photographs courtesy of Colour-Rail

Introduction

This is the seventh book in the 'Lost Lines' series. A selection of lost lines, and subjects concerning closed railways in London, has been chosen for this volume.

Although there had been some closures at the formation of the nationalised railway network in 1948, the railways of London had not seen substantial closures. There had certainly been changes as tube, tram, and road competition, together with the destruction caused by World War 2, all had their influence on London's railway network.

The 1960s saw the demolition of the Euston Doric Arch and the Beeching Report threatened to spell the end of a number of London's lines. It was during this period that I first set out to record those lines proposed for closure and I have retained a great interest in railways ever since.

London is unique in not having many great lengths of lost line, but rather many relatively short closed lines and numerous disused railway facilities, particularly relating to freight. The complexity of the London network defies easy description and as such the format of this particular volume of the 'Lost Lines' series is, by necessity, slightly different in character to the first six volumes that cover the rest of the country. Furthermore, lost lines in London covered by earlier volumes have generally not been duplicated in this book.

In the course of researching this book I have been surprised at how many former railway facilities, some taken out of operational use many years ago, still remain in the capital. Equally, although London has been relatively fortunate in that there are not too many lost lines, I found myself struck by the number of lost stations in London, particularly on lines that remain open. Well over 100 stations have been closed in the London area. I have also been surprised by the return to nature that has occurred on some sections of former railway land. A number of locations were more reminiscent of remote countryside, although in fact they were situated in the deepest metropolis.

Abbreviations

BR	British Railways
DLR	Docklands Light Railway
ECML	East Coast main line
ER	Eastern Region of British Railways
GCR	Great Central Railway
GER	Great Eastern Railway
GNR	Great Northern Railway
GWR	Great Western Railway
LBSCR	London, Brighton & South Coast Railway
LCDR	London, Chatham & Dover Railway
LMR	London Midland Region of British Railways
LMS	London, Midland & Scottish Railway
LNER	London & North Eastern Railway
LNWR	London & North Western Railway
LSWR	London & South Western Railway
LT	London Transport
LTSR	London, Tilbury & Southend Railway
Met	Metropolitan Railway
MR	Midland Railway
NLR	North London Railway
PLA	Port of London Authority
SECR	South Eastern & Chatham Railway
SER	South Eastern Railway
SR	Southern Railway
WR	Western Region of British Railways

Right: The railways arrived in London in triumphal spirit. Philip Hardwick's magnificent granite Doric Arch at the entrance to Euston station was completed in 1838. Although the most impressive railway monument in London, the LMS was the first to hatch plans to remove it. British Railways

1 The Development of a Magnificent Network

The transport potential of the London area was first recognised by the Romans. London became a port and the building of a bridge across the River Thames provided a focus for roads. The river provided links to the outside world and later a series of canals linked the Thames to other parts of the country. The first railway line in the London area was the Surrey Iron Railway which opened from Wandsworth to Croydon in 1803. This was a horse-worked mineral line that was constructed as an alternative to a canal. The next line was the London & Greenwich Railway which opened a 3¾-mile section from Spa Road, near London Bridge, to Deptford in February 1836 to become the first passenger railway in London.

From these small and isolated beginnings a series of railway lines grew into a massive network that became unprecedented anywhere else in the world. More than anything in the 19th century the railway aided the growth of London and helped to turn it into the greatest commercial centre in the world. The railways encouraged commuters to travel into the city and consequently London grew and grew. The population by 1901 had reached 6.5 million.

London developed as the capital of the British Empire and many railway companies located their headquarters, or offices, in the capital. Equally, their passenger terminal stations became London's great new cathedrals to the railway age. The development of London led to congestion and to increasing land prices. Consequently, the first underground lines in the world were built. The Metropolitan Railway, the name

shortened to 'Metro' is used worldwide to denote underground railways, ran from Bishop's Road, in the then greenfield Paddington area, to Farringdon Street in the City. It was opened in January 1863 and trains were steam-hauled before 1905.

It took a further two decades to complete the Circle Line, but tunnelling by the 'cut and cover' method caused much surface congestion. The circular shaft of a bridge foundation led to the idea of a metal 'tube' tunnel and in 1870 this form of construction was used under the River Thames from Tower Hill to near Tooley Street. This less complicated and disruptive form of circular metal tunnel construction was a prelude to the development of London's deep tube system. The first passenger electric tube line was opened from King William Street to Stockwell by the City & South London Railway in December 1890. Later an American financier, Samuel Yerkes, had considerable involvement in the development of the London tube system. 'Westbound' and 'eastbound', as opposed to 'up' and 'down', together with open carriages were a result of his influence.

A tramway system also developed and became the most extensive in the country, with dedicated routes such as the Kingsway Subway. In the early 1900s, before electrification of many of London's suburban rail services, more passengers used the trams rather than the trains. However, as the motorbus improved in reliability and costs, the tramway system declined. The last London tram ran in July 1952, with the promise that their demise would speed up the capital's traffic.

Left: An Armstrong '517' class 0-4-2T, No 1165, and a single coach arrive at the rural Trumpers Crossing Halte (note the spelling of halte), on the former broad gauge GWR branch from Southall to the Thames at Brentford. Although passenger services to this halt ended in February 1926, the line helped develop the area and is still used for some freight. Ian Allan Library

The railway network that developed in London was constructed by private companies. As such, no grand state plan or central terminus was devised. Nevertheless, a ruling in 1846 by the Royal Commission on Railway Termini prevented main line railways from entering the West End or City. There was also opposition by the Corporation of London to the construction of railways. Consequently, a number of individually designed main line termini were eventually located on the edge of the central area, linked by a network of underground lines.

In 1899 the Great Central Railway opened its London extension to Marylebone. This was to prove the last main line to reach the capital. However, this was not the end of railway development in London and new suburban lines continued to be built, up to the present day.

Above: The first passenger tube railway in the world: the gas-lit 1,430ft-long Tower Subway. Originally a single cable-hauled carriage ran along a 2ft 6in gauge track. This was not a success and the line was quickly converted into a pedestrian subway. The nearby opening of Tower Bridge led to the subway's closure in 1894. Author's collection

Right: The hugely impressive Great Hall at Euston, dating from 1849 and jointly designed by Philip Hardwick and his son Philip Charles Hardwick. The rich 61ft-wide ceiling made it the largest waiting room in the British Isles. When this view was taken in 1937 the hall had been redecorated by the LMS to the design of the eminent architect, Sir Edwin Lutyens. Topical Press

Below right: As congestion in London grew, the first underground passenger railway in the world was opened in 1863. The 'cut and cover' construction method caused considerable disturbance at street level above. Disruption was compounded on the Victoria Embankment by drainage works, as this view taken in about 1869, of work on the Metropolitan District Railway near Somerset House, shows. Copyright London Regional Transport

Left: The circular entrance to the Tower Subway at Tower Hill, dating from 1870 and viewed here in 1997. Originally a lift descended some 60ft to the line, but this was soon replaced by wooden stairs. Although closed in 1894, the metal tunnel still carries power and water mains under the Thames. Author

Below: A mass of railways were eventually constructed to serve London, as this view of the lines out of Paddington in August 1967 shows. Rationalisation and closure of the goods depot has since reduced considerably the tracks at this location. British Railways

2 Decades of Destruction

By the turn of the century amalgamations had resulted in about a dozen major pre-Grouping main line companies serving the capital. The impact of the motorbus, the electric tram and tube, the car and the lorry all made inroads into their profitability. They were further weakened by neglect during World War 1. Consequently, in 1923 the main line companies were grouped into what were known as the 'Big Four' railway companies. They were the London, Midland & Scottish; London & North Eastern; Southern, and Great Western railways, all of which had their headquarters in London.

Rationalisation also took place on the underground lines. The General Strike in 1926 and the slump of 1929-31 did nothing to improve the financial prospects of railways in London. Although large numbers were using the system, competition kept fares low and the return on investment was poor. By 1915 there were two main operators in London, the Underground Group and London County Council. The advantages of integration led them to come together in 1933 to establish the London Passenger Transport Board. Although this excluded the main line railways, it did create the biggest transport monopoly in the London area and London Transport was effectively set up at this time.

World War 2 was to have a profound effect on the capital's railways. In September 1939 the Government took over both London Transport and the main line railways. London suffered in the intensive air-raids (the Blitz) and many stations and sections of line were destroyed, some never to be reopened. Damage was particularly severe in London's East End, but the destruction of railway installations was widespread. Even the offices of the London Necropolis Railway, a company that conveyed London's dead to Brookwood Cemetery, were destroyed.

The rundown state of the railways after World War 2 resulted in their nationalisation. In 1948 London Transport became an executive of the British Transport Commission. The Commission was also responsible for the main line railways in London, but unlike London Transport, these lines were divided between four regions run by British Railways.

Although London has few long stretches of closed railway, much of the capital was once rail-connected in one way or another, and many short sections of line and former rail links have been lost. There have been closures over many years, but the first of any significance date back to World War 1. Damage during World War 2 resulted in losses and there was some rationalisation in the 1950s. Yet the 1960s were to see the railways in London reach their lowest ebb. At that time modernism was all the vogue; the railways and their Victorian architecture were old fashioned, almost despised. The destruction of the Euston Arch epitomised the fall; there were even plans to close St Pancras.

In 1962 the British Transport Commission was abolished and the new British Railways Board, with

Right: Much damage was caused by World War 2. This view shows the bomb-ruined and roofless repair shop at New Cross Gate after official closure, but with two locomotives in various states of disrepair, on 29 June 1947. S. Nash

Left: This view shows the last 54 tram service leaving the Victoria tram terminus for New Cross Gate. This was one of the tram routes changed over to bus operation in a two-year tram to bus conversion that led up to the last London tram running in 1952. Topical Press

Below left: Cannon Street station opened in 1866. Hawkshaw was the engineer, with hotel designs by E. M. Barry. The station remains, but this view shows demolition of the great roof in progress in 1958. 'Schools' class 4-4-0 No 30920 is at the head of the 4.44pm express to Ramsgate, while on the next road is a Hastings diesel-electric unit.
P. Ransome-Wallis

Dr Beeching at its helm, produced the infamous Reshaping Report. This report identified a number of lines for passenger closure in the London area. These included the route from Barking to Kentish Town, together with the (already closed) Palace Gates branch. Broad Street to Richmond, and Clapham Junction to Kensington Olympia were among the longer stretches of route identified for closure. Branches from Harrow to Belmont, Watford Junction to both Croxley Green and St Albans, together with the lines from West Drayton to both Uxbridge Vine Street (already closed) and Staines West were included. The links from Woodside to Selsdon, and from Romford to Upminster were also earmarked for closure.

Yet the peak use of lines remained high and even the Beeching Report recognised that the suburban services in London came close to covering their costs, but that peak capacity was limited and fares were too low to finance costly improvements. There was mounting concern that the closure of lines should be contemplated at all in such a congested city. Indeed a section of the North London Line, threatened with closure in the Beeching Report, carried over 18,000 passengers a day. Commuting by train was on the increase and commuters were moving further out.

A fightback began to emerge. The 1968 Transport Act introduced grant provisions for rail services. The oil crisis of 1973, and growing road congestion, meant that only a part of the Beeching proposals were ever implemented in London. The lines which closed completely were the branches to Uxbridge Vine Street, Staines West, Belmont, Palace Gates and the link between Woodside and Selsdon. The link from Dalston to Broad Street was also eventually closed.

In 1992 British Rail was restructured into business sectors, and Network South East incorporated all the main line railways in the London area. Privatisation was to follow, and this saw the return of private companies serving the capital. Meanwhile, London Transport, after a period under the management of the Greater London Council, was brought back under Government control and renamed London Regional Transport. Although a stop has been put on further significant closures in London, as this book shows, some sections of line continue to be lost.

Nevertheless, more lines are being opened than closed and the decline has at last ended. Just as pollution of the River Thames once prompted great public health infrastructure improvements, a growing awareness of car pollution and congestion is prompting improvements to the railways in the capital. New lines and stations are being built. Buildings that obstructed closed lines have been demolished to make way for reopenings; even the tram is back. London's railways are at the dawn of a new age. We may even see the extraction of the remains of the Euston Doric arch from its murky resting place on the bed of the River Lea. The fact that its restoration is being pursued at all confirms that the decades of destruction are over.

Above: Although frequent damage was inflicted on London during World War 2, 1962 saw continued destruction with the removal of the historic Doric Arch at Euston, which dated from 1837. Even the demolition contractor offered to store the arch, but those in charge at the time would have none of it. British Railways

Below: Hardwick's Great Hall at Euston. Completed in 1849, the solid classical grandeur of the hall and the historic first railway hotel in the world were being demolished when this view was taken in 1963. Acts of destruction that history now seriously questions. British Railways

Above: Old railway landmarks were destroyed all over the capital in the 1960s. This view is of the site of Platforms 14 and 15 and the Cardington Street Dining Club, at Euston station, during demolition in 1963. British Railways

Left: Even smaller stations that remained open were demolished, as this view of the destruction of the former Midland Railway buildings at Mill Hill Broadway, in May 1964, shows. Ian Allan Library

Below left: The flying viaduct link from Point Pleasant Junction to East Putney was opened by the LSWR in July 1889. Regular passenger services ceased over the main viaduct in 1941. The former LSWR line to Wimbledon is now mainly used by District Line trains, but a connection between the two lines still exists to the right of this view, which was taken in April 1998. Author

Right: Broad Street station dated from 1865 and was once an attractive mixture of Italian and oriental styles, crowned with a clock tower. However, after years of neglect and disfigurement it became easier to justify demolition. This view shows all that was left on 10 October 1985, as the station gave way to the new Broadgate development. M. J. Stretton

Far right: After a fight with conservationists it was decided to retain much of Liverpool Street station, rather than demolish almost all of the Gothic-styled station as had been originally proposed. This view in 1989 shows excavation work so that Platforms 1-8 could be brought into line with the new concourse. The change in approach at Liverpool Street, and the success of the completed station, marked the end of a particularly destructive period for London's railways.
E. Godward

Above: A view taken in 1954 of the clock tower and offices at Liverpool Street station, with Broad Street station in the background. The disposition of buildings once allowed connection between the GER and the Metropolitan Railway at this point and small parts of the old connecting tunnel, which was last used in 1904, remain. Damage in World War 2 resulted in the removal of much of the roof at Broad Street and a spire that once capped the clock tower at Liverpool Street. However, after World War 2 all the buildings in this particular view were demolished by British Railways. British Railways

③ A Geographical Perspective

London originated from its generally favourable transport location. The River Thames could be crossed here and main roads converged on London, as later did the canals. The expansion of the port and the development of industry combined to create a vast metropolis.

Yet the railways were by far the biggest single influence on development. London eventually became the centre of a spider's web of railway lines. The development of dormitory suburbs was made possible by the railway. Cheap fares and intensive services allowed almost unlimited expansion of the capital. A range of other issues — the geology, the destruction of World War 2, planning policies, including the constraints of the Green Belt — were all to mould the structure of the city, but none had more influence than the railway.

Physically central London is in an artesian basin. Higher land to the north and south at one time allowed the fountains in Trafalgar Square to operate without any form of pumping. This topography required the railways to build tunnels to both the north and south of the city, but did not seriously interfere with railway construction. Also at the centre of London is the River Thames, which provided an expensive barrier to north/south communications for main line railways. Equally, the division created a distinct character to the railways north and south of the river.

Much of the geology of the area allowed for relatively easy construction of tube railways. This was particularly so north of the river, where a layer of blue clay provided an almost ideal medium for tunnelling tube lines. Building underground also saved on land prices, which were traditionally high in the city. The high cost of land also resulted in much of the surface network being constructed on viaducts.

Where London finishes is a matter of debate. London has developed from many individual settlements and comprises many parts, including the small area of the City of London itself. The physical area covered by urban development is one guide, the administrative area covered by the London Boroughs, another.

In choosing topics for this book I have made an arbitrary choice myself, considering that some lines, that are well outside the capital, have closer associations with London than others. In railway terms this has always been the case. Indeed early maps of London Transport stretch out some 30 miles to Luton and Guildford. This administrative area has since been reduced, until only the former Ongar line terminated deep in a rural area.

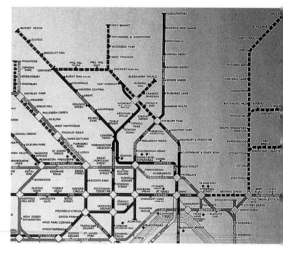

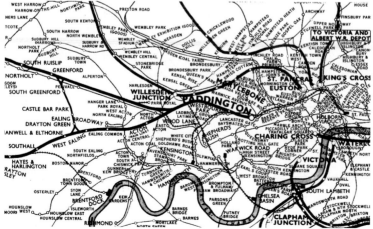

Above: Extract from map of the London Underground and proposed new lines in 1939. Copyright London Regional Transport

Left: Map of the western sector of London, from a Western Region poster of 1958. Author's collection

4 Change on the City Line

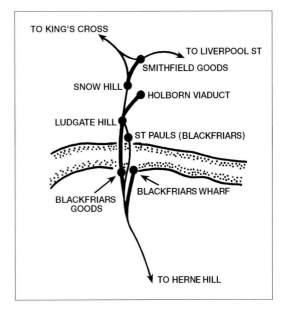

The Corporation of London discouraged the railway. There had been protest about the disfigurement of Ludgate Hill with a railway bridge, yet one of the most enduring images of London was a view looking up Ludgate Hill towards St Paul's Cathedral, a view obscured by a bridge carrying the City Line from Farringdon to Herne Hill. The bridge has since been removed, and the line, after a period of closure, has been rebuilt underground. Personally, I considered the bridge, with the arms of the City of London emblazoned on its side, complemented the scene rather well. Nevertheless, I accept that the storage of empty stock and the nearby derelict shell of Ludgate Hill station were perhaps not entirely fitting to the City's image.

The 4½-mile line of the former London, Chatham & Dover Railway ran from Herne Hill to what were known as the Metropolitan's Widened Lines at Farringdon. The route was expensive to construct, but allowed cross-London workings. The line first opened from the Elephant and Castle to a temporary terminus on the south side of the River Thames, called Blackfriars Bridge, in June 1864. The Thames was bridged by December 1864 and the line extended to Ludgate Hill, a permanent station being completed here by June of the following year. On the opening of the line crossing the Thames, the temporary terminus at Blackfriars Bridge became part of a freight depot. However, this was such a small depot that the marshalling of trains had to be carried out at sorting sidings near Herne Hill. The section from Ludgate Hill, north to Farringdon, was opened in January 1866. In September 1871 an eastward connecting spur was also provided to the Widened Lines. A short branch from the Ludgate-Farringdon section of line opened to Holborn Viaduct in March 1874. In August of the

same year an intermediate station at Snow Hill was opened on the City Line.

Both passenger and freight traffic developed, and in May 1886 a second parallel bridge across the Thames was opened. This provided a loop off the original line and ran via a new station called St Paul's, which was renamed Blackfriars in 1937. The loop joined the original through route, just south of Ludgate Hill station.

Below: Ludgate Hill station, viewed from the steeple of St Bride's Church in Fleet Street, when an overall roof graced the attractive brickwork of the station. On the left of this view the bridge over Ludgate Hill itself can be seen. In 1863 a petition against the construction of this bridge raised over 1,000 signatures. Author's collection

The electric tram and tube reduced much of the line's passenger traffic. The Ludgate Hill to Victoria services, together with Snow Hill station (which had been renamed Holborn Viaduct Low Level in 1912) closed during World War 1. Ludgate Hill station, which was exceedingly close to Blackfriars, was closed in March 1929, but remained as a disused shell for many more years. The connecting spur running eastwards from Snow Hill to the Widened Lines was last used in 1927, but the tunnel itself was not demolished until 1958.

Through freight services continued to be important and in the early 1960s almost 100 freight trains a day used the route. However, a decline in freight also set in. Goods services which had been provided for Smithfield Market since 1869, when it was the largest cattle market in the world, were used for the last time in July 1962. The freight depot at Blackfriars closed for most services in 1965 and the disused wharf on the river was demolished.

Worse was to come; the line beyond Blackfriars was closed completely in March 1969 and the track removed. In 1971 the original Thames bridge was taken out of use and the decking was demolished in 1985. The history of this bridge is outlined in the Southern volume of the 'Lost Lines' series.

Fortunately, the subterranean part of the closed route remained free from obstruction and the line was rebuilt and reopened. Today, the section beyond Blackfriars dives below Ludgate Hill on a partly new route to Farringdon, the old shell of Ludgate Hill station has at last been demolished and the area redeveloped. Surprisingly perhaps, being so close to the City, part of the original Blackfriars freight station on the southern bank of the Thames remains, together with its original cobbled entrance.

Left: Snow Hill station opened in 1874 and was known as Holborn Viaduct Low Level from 1912. This view is taken from the station's platform with a freight train from the LNER to the SR, headed by Class N1 0-6-2T No 4565, on 4 April 1933. The gradient in the southbound direction, up to Blackfriars Bridge, was steep enough to warrant a banking engine to be permanently used on this section of line. O. J. Morris

Below left: A Gresley-designed Class J50 0-6-0T, No 68913, on a freight train bound for Hither Green passes the long-derelict Snow Hill station, which closed to passengers in 1916 and is seen here on 29 April 1954. R. C. Riley

Above: Snow Hill station viewed from the north on 19 January 1984 after abandonment of the line. The remains of the signalbox can just be made out in the foreground. At one time the future of this route looked very bleak. British Railways

Above right: Old Seacole Lane Bridge, looking towards Blackfriars on 19 January 1984. The Seacole name is derived from the fact that many years ago, before the river became silted up, barges from the northeast berthed on the east bank of the Fleet to discharge their coal in this area. British Railways

Right: Holborn Viaduct with the new station building in the background. The little-used water tank on the right can just be seen adjacent to Platform 1 in this early 1960s view. R. J. Marshall

Below: Snow Hill Tunnel, with Holborn Viaduct station on the right. The terminus, which opened in March 1874, was located at the end of a short 292yd spur from Ludgate Hill Junction and is seen here on 13 September 1984. B. Morrison

Above: The scene at Holborn Viaduct on 18 August 1989 as the dome of the Old Bailey slowly vanishes from view behind the development to the rear. In Platform 1, Class 415/4 No 5478 leads the 16.33 service for Orpington. The station closed in January of the following year. B. Morrison

Below: A Class 2 2-6-2T, No 40026, is about to pass over Ludgate Hill bridge with a freight train for the Widened Lines in 1962. The bridge obscured views of St Paul's when viewed from Fleet Street, but was attractively embellished with the City of London's arms. The damage caused during World War 2 to this part of London was still apparent from the foreground of this view. L. Sandler

Right: The remains of Ludgate Hill station are seen here in January 1984. The station was last used for passenger services in 1929. The restricted size of the station is apparent. When in use an island platform was provided between the two outer walls. These walls at one time supported an overall roof. British Railways

Centre right: Infrastructure was cut back. The original Blackfriars railway bridge over the River Thames, dating from 1864, is seen here being demolished in June 1984. The bridge was taken out of use primarily because of the reduction in freight traffic over the route. One of the abutments, that carried the crest of the London, Chatham & Dover Railway and the bridge's opening date of 1864, was retained and restored. British Railways

Below: The cast-iron river piers of the first Blackfriars railway bridge remain in 1998. The piers were built on stones from the old Westminster road bridge, which was demolished shortly before the opening of the rail bridge in 1864. Plans to use a line of former bridge piers to carry a new platform for Blackfriars station have been considered. Author

Below right: The remains of one of the old freight facilities at Blackfriars on the south side of the River Thames. The freight depot, which for a time operated a Grande Vitesse service for Continental traffic, closed in 1964 and this view was taken in September 1997. Author

5 The Forgotten Freight Yards

London acted as a focus for railway freight, and goods yards were provided throughout the city. Coal traffic was considerable and major firms and markets also had their own depots, such as Cadbury. Decline came over many years, with perhaps a glimpse of things to come when the Midland Railway closed Whitecross Street in 1935, and the Metropolitan Railway closed its Farringdon Street freight depot the following year. Today the general freight depots in central London have all closed, providing in many cases huge potential for redevelopment. Consideration of all the London facilities would involve a book in itself, but some of the major lost sites of interest are as follows:

Paddington

Paddington freight yard was located on the site of the original 1838 passenger station. A history of the yard, which closed in stages between 1972 and 1975, was detailed in the Western volume of 'Lost Lines'. The GWR had other freight yards in London which served all parts of the city. The main yards were at Acton, Brentford, Park Royal, Smithfield, South Lambeth and Victoria & Albert in Docklands. Smaller depots also existed. Amongst those located in west London were Westbourne Park, Warwick Road, Chelsea, Old Oak Common, Shepherd's Bush and Hammersmith.

Left: Cadbury's London depot at Finchley Road, with an ex-Midland Railway Johnson Class 2 0-6-0 shunting in the 1930s. MacFisheries, and many other businesses and markets had dedicated rail depots in London before large scale transfer to road haulage. Topical Press

Above: A former Eastern Region 'Goods & Coal Depot' dark-blue enamel sign. Rail-freight depots were once a common sight in London, but this sign, seen here in September 1997, is now confined to the railway museum at North Woolwich station. Author

Below left: A view in September 1997 looking towards Bishop's Bridge Road and the entrance to the former Paddington goods depot which was closed in stages by 1975. At this point, only a police hut and the lower entrance to the once expansive freight depot remains. Author

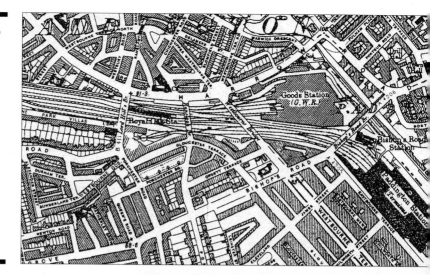

Right: Map of the freight facilities to the north of Paddington station in 1938. Crown copyright

Centre right: The Regent's Canal at the former Marylebone Wharf. Interchange between the Great Central Railway and the canal was once provided here and the wall of the freight wharf was still visible when this view was taken in September 1997. Author

Below right: Map of the various freight facilities at Marylebone in 1938. Crown copyright

Marylebone

In 1898 coal trains ran over the Great Central Railway extension to Marylebone, where a separate coal yard was provided. A 35-ton Goliath electric crane was used in the general goods yard, which was located to the northeast of the coal yard. The third facility was a wharf for interchange of freight with the Regent's Canal. General freight to Marylebone ended in 1952 and the coal yard closed in 1965. A goods shed was used as a parcel depot until 1967. Today the sites have been given over to housing and little remains, but parts of the Regent's Canal wharf can still be seen.

St Pancras and Somers Town

St Pancras goods yard was located some way north of the passenger station and opened in 1865. A further freight depot was opened in 1877 to the west of St Pancras station itself and was known as Somers Town. As with St Pancras passenger station, Somers Town was designed by Sir Gilbert Scott and the bricks were especially made of differing sizes: smaller bricks being used higher on the walls to give an added impression of sturdiness. At one time, Somers Town was developed as a potato and vegetable depot, but in the 1960s was operated in conjunction with the other facilities at St Pancras, including the beer vaults. During this period about 14 freight trains a day included Glasgow, Sheffield, Leeds and Burton upon Trent as destinations. Freight to the St Pancras goods sites ceased by 1975 and much of the Somers Town site is now given over to the New British Library.

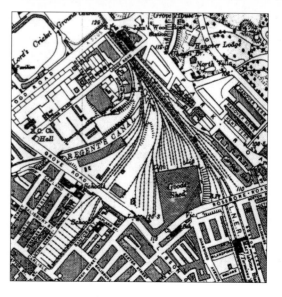

Haydon Square

Other freight depots once operated by the LMR included the former LNWR depots at Camden and Haydon Square. The latter was one of a number of depots, including those at Mint Street, Commercial Road and London Docks that were all located near Fenchurch Street station on the former LTSR line. Facilities at Haydon Square were closed in 1962 and transferred to

Above left: The Somers Town wholesale potato depot was located immediately to the west of St Pancras station. Designed by Sir Gilbert Scott, in a red-brick Gothic style, it was a functional building far less ornate than the Midland Grand Hotel opposite. The view here was in early LMS days. Ian Allan library

Below left: Gothic-style walls to the former Somers Town goods depot, viewed here in September 1997. The design was such that smaller bricks were placed higher up the wall to give the structure a perception of greater solidity. Somers Town Low Level depot closed in June 1967 and the Phoenix Street depot closed the following April. Author

Above: A notice announcing the closure of Haydon Square goods depot on 2 July 1962. The alternative facilities, offered at Broad Street, closed in 1969.
David Lawrence

Broad Street, until this also closed in 1969. All the depots are now closed, but some interesting remains can be found at Camden and Mint Street.

King's Cross

An extensive area to the north of King's Cross station was provided by the Great Northern Railway for freight traffic, together with the Maiden Lane area which was used by the North London Railway. The GNR area was linked to the Regent's Canal, which gave access to the Thames. Coal, livestock and vegetables were all once handled in large quantities. In the 1960s about 25 freight trains a day provided services to main centres in the north and to Scotland. Freightliners used the site of the former engine shed from 1966. Closure of part of the freight area came in 1967 and the main King's Cross goods depot closed in March 1973. In 1988 many of the buildings were in an advanced state of dilapidation pending redevelopment,

but there remains some rail-freight activity to the north of the site.

Bishopsgate and Spitalfields

The original passenger station at Bishopsgate was rebuilt by Sancton Wood. It was opened by the Eastern Counties Railway in July 1840 and was simply called London. Bishopsgate closed with the opening of Liverpool Street in November 1875 and in 1881 it was rebuilt as a goods depot. A fire led to its closure in December 1964, after which it was demolished. Much of the site has been derelict, or used for car parking for many years, but there are proposals for redevelopment. The Spitalfields depot, which was located just east of Bishopsgate, closed in November 1967.

Temple Mills Hump Yard

Temple Mills was developed in order to rationalise activity at about a dozen separate goods yards,

Right: Map of the freight facilities and mass of lines that were provided at St Pancras and at King's Cross in 1938. Crown copyright

Below: The crumbling white-brick coal office at King's Cross in June 1997. The offices backed onto the Regent's Canal and the freight yard at one time provided interchange facilities. Although a number of temporary uses have been found for some of the former freight buildings to the north of King's Cross station, many remain derelict, such as these offices viewed here in September 1977. Author

Above left: The Great Northern Railway provided a number of huge warehouses on its network. King's Cross was no exception, as shown in this view taken in September 1997 of one of the few buildings in the King's Cross freight area remaining in good condition. At one time about 300 horses were employed on the site and were mainly used for delivery purposes. Most rail freight ended in March 1973. Author

Left: A sinister-looking subway beckoned to Bishopsgate from the old Liverpool Street station. Viewed here in 1964, it remained a modest walk from the end of the subway to the old Bishopsgate station. Author

Above: An attractive double arch at the former goods depot at Bishopsgate. The 1849 station was designed by Sancton Wood and was constructed above this viaduct. Much of the station was later converted for use as a bonded warehouse, with large amounts of spirits being stored from the Continent. The building caught fire on 6 December 1964 and two customs officials were killed in the blaze. After the fire, the damage was so extensive that the main building had to be demolished. Author

Below left: At Spitalfields, to the east of Bishopsgate, a goods depot was provided to serve the nearby fruit and vegetable market. A wagon hoist gave access to the East London Line. The depot was last used in November 1967, but derelict platform awnings and track inlaid in cobbles still remained at the site in September 1997, when this view was taken. Author

Below: The iron gates to the lower part of Bishopsgate at the front entrance to the old station. The gates still contain the crest of the Great Eastern Railway. When this view was taken in September 1997 some of the land formerly utilised by the station was used for car parking, but there are plans to redevelop the site. Author

Right: Map of the freight facilities at Bishopsgate station, including those at Broad Street in 1938.
Crown copyright

Below: Temple Mills, when viewed here in January 1959, was a modern, fully-mechanised marshalling yard, designed to speed freight movements and facilitate the sorting of wagons into train loads. The yard, which automatically was able to control wagon speeds in shunting operations, virtually did the work formerly carried out in about a dozen yards. British Railways

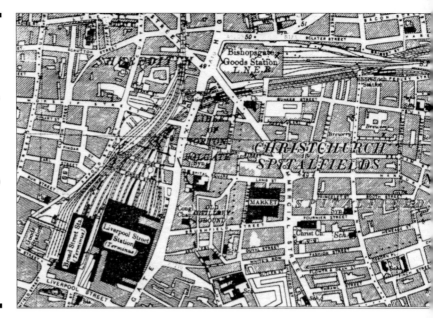

including those at Goodmayes, Thames Wharf and Mile End. The task of creating a new yard started in 1954 and took almost five years to complete. Temple Mills was a 'hump yard' with the capacity to handle 100 trains a day on its 50 sorting sidings. Almost as soon as it was completed wagon-load freight declined and the increasing use of block trains brought into question the yard's relevance. No longer used as a hump yard for general freight, parts are still used as an engineers' depot. Indeed, even the freightliner depot at Stratford was unused in 1998, with the huge container cranes being mothballed.

Battersea Wharf, South Lambeth and Nine Elms

Battersea Wharf was sited on the River Thames, between Battersea Park and the power station. It was located on part of the area of the original Pimlico passenger station, which closed in 1860. Just as Battersea Power station obtained its supplies of coal by sea, the railway wharf was also served by barges, known as lighters, from the main docks. The LBSCR developed the wharf as one of its main coal depots. The area remained in use for freight until its closure in May 1970. Just down the line from Battersea, the GWR had its South Lambeth depot. This substantial depot, the only one operated south of the river by the GWR, opened in 1913 and closed in November 1980.

Nine Elms once provided an extensive freight area with connections to the Thames. Originally the

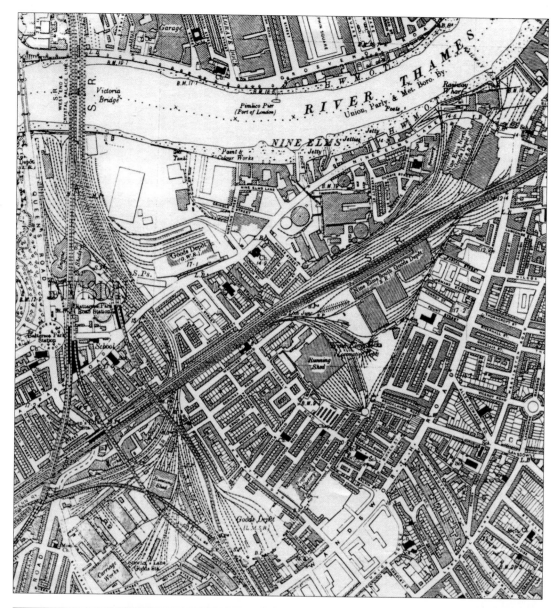

Above left: Although there remains some rail activity in the Temple Mills area, the hump yard itself is no longer used for general freight and in September 1997, when this view was taken, the site and surroundings were but a shadow of their former glory. Author

Left: Battersea Wharf can be seen in the front of this view, taken in May 1970. Buses had already replaced the coal sidings after final closure of the depot. Coal once arrived here on Thames barges. The power station at Battersea also received most of its coal by sea and at this time, before it was phased out in the 1970s, was still belching its smoke and steam into the London air. C. Gifford

Above: Map of the mass of railway lines, depots and sheds on the south side of the River Thames in 1938. Crown copyright

LSWR's London passenger terminus, Nine Elms was first used as a freight depot with the opening of Waterloo station in 1848. It was closed in 1968 and traffic was diverted to South Lambeth.

Bricklayers Arms

A terminal station was opened at Bricklayers Arms by the South Eastern and London & Croydon railways in May 1844. The original passenger station had a facade by Lewis Cubitt and was built largely to avoid tolls for the use of London Bridge station. However, it was not well sited and closed to regular passengers in January 1852. The site was subsequently used for freight, with sheep and cattle traffic being important. Fire damaged the original station and the remains were demolished in

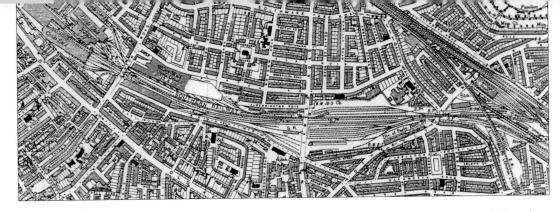

1936, although passenger excursions were not finally phased out until 1939. Freight lasted longer, indeed a parcels depot was opened in 1969 and remained in use until 1981. An engineering depot ended rail use of the site in October 1983. The site has subsequently been redeveloped, but some features, in particular a number of distinctive walls, remain.

Feltham

Feltham was built by the LSWR in 1921-2 and in the construction of the yard considerable use was made of concrete. It was particularly important during World War 2, as it enabled freight to avoid London. However, operations gradually declined as wagon loads dwindled and the yard closed in September 1968. The main control building, with its clock tower, remained as a derelict shell until it was demolished in the mid-1990s. Today some buildings still remain on the site, together with fragments of lamps, track fittings and even the odd brake block. The concrete subways, under what was once a mass of sidings, also remain. Finally of interest, a short freight line also once ran from Feltham to serve an industrial area north of the yard.

Above: Map of the elongated Bricklayers Arms and Willow Walk sites in 1938. Crown copyright

Below: The substantial track layout at Bricklayers Arms was crossed by a number of extensive bridges. This disused bridge, viewed here in September 1997 and to the east of the main yard, had been renewed before closure took place. Author

Below right: The Bricklayers Arms and Willow Walk depots merged in 1932. 'The Brick' was finally abandoned in 1981 and has since been redeveloped. Nevertheless, a few items of the former railway yard remained in 1998, including part of the boundary walls and a warning that overhead electric wires were used here. The Southern's ground-level electric third-rail was potentially hazardous in shunting yards. Author

Above: The River Crane flowed under Feltham yard and a substantial flat arch was provided to ease the river's flow in the event of flooding. The arch, when viewed here in September 1997, looked rather sinister. Author's collection

Right: There had been no use of Feltham yard since it closed in September 1968, when this view was taken almost 30 years later. Although most of the concrete buildings have been demolished, some remain in a derelict condition. A number of subways, that once provided safe access for staff under the sidings, also remain. One such disused subway is seen here in September 1997. Author's collection

Below: A freight train leaves the west end of Feltham yard, headed by a Urie 'S15' 4-6-0 with a down working. A diesel shunter in its original livery, No 13042, stands by in the open on 7 July 1954. L. King

⑥ Two Tunnels to the Strand

The Aldwych Shuttle

The Brompton & Piccadilly Circus Railway and the Great Northern & Strand Railway merged to become the Great Northern, Piccadilly & Brompton Railway. A connecting line from Piccadilly Circus to Holborn, to link the two railways, left the proposed original southern terminus of the Great Northern & Strand Railway at the Strand, as a short spur off the new main line. The Piccadilly Line, as it became known, was opened between Finsbury Park and Hammersmith in December 1906, but the short ⅓-mile spur from Holborn to the Strand did not open until November 1907. The branch line was known as the Strand Extension. A shuttle service ran from 5.40am to beyond midnight and on opening about a million passengers a year used the branch. There was even a through late-night train for the benefit of theatre users.

Strand station was renamed Aldwych in 1915. However, only one of the two single-line tunnels was used and with just a two-car set using the line and a peak hour service being introduced, the first call for closure came in 1933. The branch was closed in September 1940 for the duration of World War 2 and

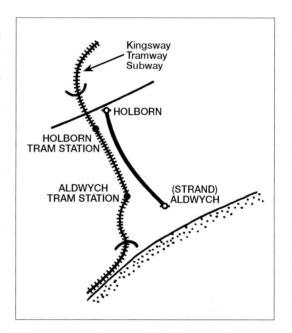

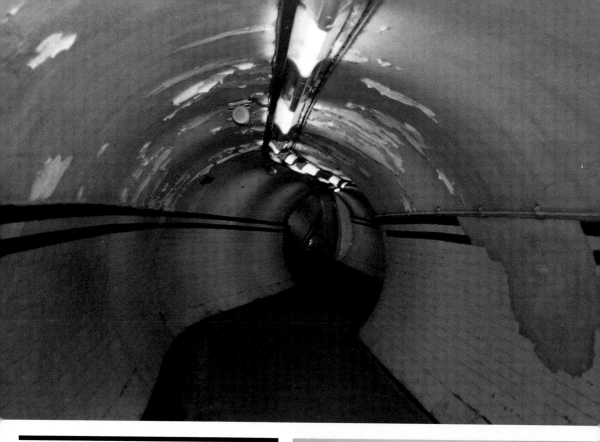

Left: Opened in 1907, to a standard design developed by Leslie Green, and having changed little during its operational lifetime, Aldwych station's main entrance and exit onto Surrey Street is viewed here on the last day of passenger operation, Friday 30 September 1994. Author

Above: The dilapidated state of Aldwych station was evident from this view of one of the subways leading to the platforms on the last day of passenger services in 1994. During World War 2 the station was closed and used as an air-raid shelter, whilst the branch tunnels were used to store treasures from the British Museum. Author

Centre right: At Holborn, Platform 5 was used by the Aldwych shuttle trains. This view was taken on Friday 30 September 1994, the last day of operation before closure. During World War 2 this platform was used as an office. Author

Below right: Although the station was renamed Aldwych in 1915, the original Strand name remained in the platform tiling until the line closed, as this view taken in September 1994 shows. Author

Left: After closure, the street level facilities at Aldwych station were used for an exhibition of paintings by Charles Avery, as this view taken in September 1997 shows. Author

Above: Poster boards remain unused in Aldwych station when this view was taken in September 1997. Had plans proceeded to extend the Jubilee Line via Aldwych, rather than on its present route, the station would have probably still been in use. Author

Right: The last regular passenger train prepares to leave Aldwych for Holborn on Friday 30 September 1994, almost 87 years after the opening of the line. Author

Below right: When Aldwych station was used temporarily for an art exhibition, even the expansive toilets were reopened, as this view of the main booking hall taken in September 1997 shows. Author

Aldwych station was used as an air-raid shelter. Up to 1,500 persons used the station at night and important items from the British Museum, including the Elgin Marbles, were stored in the tunnels. In July 1946 the branch reopened.

The line was never intended to be the short spur that it eventually became. As far back as 1902 there had been proposals to extend the line to Temple, but there were objections to the building works. In 1905 there were plans to extend the route, via a single tunnel under the Thames to York Road at Waterloo, but there appears to have been insufficient finance. In February 1959 London Transport intended to close the Aldwych branch, but the proposal was refused. A scheme was promoted again in 1965 to connect the branch to Waterloo. There were also proposals for an extension from the Bakerloo Line to connect with the Aldwych spur. Unfortunately all schemes that may have kept the branch alive came to nothing.

Prior to closure, 37 Monday to Friday departures ran as the Aldwych Shuttle in a peak hour service that operated between 7.30am and 10am and from 3.50pm to 6.30pm. These services were not underused, but after considerable opposition a decision was made to close the line and this was implemented in September 1994. The station at Aldwych had become run-down and replacement lifts were given as a deciding factor in closing the route.

On Friday 30 September 1994 the last train contained a mixture of those who wished to pay their respects and those who wanted it to be a jolly affair with balloons and laughter. Certainly this was a unique event as there can be few capital cities of London's size and congestion, anywhere in the world, that have closed tube lines in their very heart in the 1990s. In September 1997 the station was used temporarily for an art exhibition, the toilets were reopened and one of the lifts was turned into a bar. The platforms remain, and I wager that at some future time trains will again be rumbling through the tunnels to Aldwych.

The Kingsway Subway

At the turn of the century, consideration was given to providing greater connection between the tramway lines of north and south London. Construction of a tunnel between Holborn and Aldwych for single-deck cars was seen as an answer. In February 1906 the Kingsway Subway, as it was known, opened between Holborn and Aldwych and by 1908 had been extended to the Strand.

The subway was closed in 1930 for enlargement to accommodate the standard double-deck London tram. It reopened in January 1931 and 5,000 trams a week used the subway at this time. However, after World War 2 it was decided to abandon the entire London tram network and on 5 April 1952 the last tram used the subway. Part of the subway was reopened in January 1964, having been adapted to take road traffic.

Above: E/3 type double-deck London trams emerging and entering the Kingsway Tramway Subway from the Waterloo Bridge exit. The subway, which once connected the network of tram lines to the north and south of London, boasted its own subterranean tram stations at Holborn and Aldwych.
Ian Allan Library

Below: The northern entrance to the Kingsway Tramway Subway, seen here in March 1998. In the 1930s London had one of the largest tramway systems in the world, but in 1952 it was closed down. Remarkably the original conduit tram tracks (the conduit in the middle housed two electric conductor rails) remain along this part of the subway, just as they were when the last tram left, all those years ago. Author

LONDON UNDERGROUND ⊖ LONDON UNDERGROUND ⊖

ALDWYCH

✳110✳　　　　　　　0504 30

　　　　　　　003089

C SINGLE 1803 FRI**30SEP94**　50P

ject to conditions of issue　Subject to conditions of issue Su

Right: This view was taken in 1890 of the 20-ton hydraulic lift at Stockwell, the other end of the original tube line from King William Street. The lift enabled rolling stock to be brought to the surface for repairs. Ian Allan Library

7 King William Street

The City of London & Southwark Subway Company had its terminus in the City, at 46 King William Street. The engineer for the line was James Greathead. Work began in 1886 and spoil from the twin underground tunnels was transported away by using the nearby River Thames. It was bravely decided to operate the line by electric locomotives, rather than the original idea of cable haulage. Consequently, on the station's opening in December 1890 by the Prince of Wales, later to become King Edward VII, London's first electric tube line was born. Over 10,000 passengers used the station on its first day and a surprisingly intensive service was provided. Trains ran every 5min on weekdays and a Sunday service started in 1891. The electric locomotives pulled three carriages, which because of their high upholstered sides became known as 'padded cells'. The line with its single-class, 2d fares became known as the 'Twopenny Tube'. The line prospered; King William Street was well used and very soon 15,000 passengers a day were using the route.

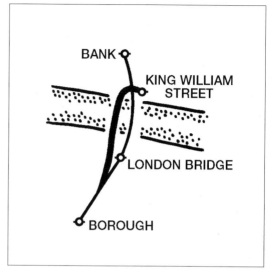

Above: Electric locomotive No 5 is seen here and was one of 14 built for the opening of the City & South London Railway in 1890. No 13, a similar locomotive, is preserved.
Locomotive Publishing Co

At King William Street station, two hydraulic lifts served the gas-lit terminus. Originally, two platforms either side of a single track were provided, but the station was modified in 1895 to a single-island platform with two tracks, each of which could accommodate the three-coach trains.

To avoid paying easement fees the underground line followed the street pattern above. This resulted in a very awkward stretch of track, that required a 1 in 14 gradient on leaving King William Street station. It proved equally difficult to extend the line northward and when an extension to the railway was proposed the opportunity was taken to provide an entirely new line which left the original north of Borough. When this through line opened in February 1900, it resulted in the closure of King William Street and the tunnels to it.

During World War 1 police raided the deserted station in a search for German spies, but found nothing. The station buildings above ground were demolished in 1933. The deserted tunnels under the Thames were sealed up during World War 2 with substantial concrete bulkheads to avoid any risk of flooding. The remaining sections were used as air-raid shelters and later for storage.

Some parts of the original station and line have remained unused for almost a century. Indeed, for many years after closure signals and signalling equipment also lingered on. Electric engine No 13 has been preserved together with one of the original coaches, although a second preserved locomotive, displayed at Moorgate, was destroyed in a World War 2 air-raid.

The naming of the station and its opening by royalty is of interest. The last King William died in 1837. The railways played no part in his funeral arrangements, but on the death of Victoria they did. Her body, as with subsequent monarchs, was brought to London by train. In September 1997 tube lines were to play their part in conveying a million people to pay their respects to Diana, Princess of Wales. After a funeral service at Westminster Abbey, Prince William arrived at Euston station and the Royal Train departed, hauled by two sparkling Class 47s, one of which was called *Prince William*. Just as the builders of King William Street station could hardly have anticipated its short life, royal destiny is equally uncertain.

Above: Exterior of the 'padded cell' cars used on the line. They acquired this notoriety because the upholstery ran up the walls to small opaque lights. Access to the 32 seats was by an open platform and a door at each end. Dating from 1890, the coaches ran in service until 1925. A surviving example is open to inspection at the London Transport Museum. Copyright London Regional Transport

Right: King William Street terminus showing the remains of the island platform and original gas lighting after closure of the station in February 1900. In 1940 the tunnel was converted into an air-raid shelter. Copyright London Regional Transport

Below right: The way out to the two hydraulically-operated lifts which ran in a single shaft up to 46 King William Street above. This view was taken some time after closure of the station. After closure, the street-level buildings in King William Street became a shop, before the building was demolished in 1933. Copyright London Regional Transport

Above: The brick tunnel just beyond the King William Street terminus, after closure, showing the start of the iron tunnels leading under the Thames and the remains of a semaphore signal. A number of original glass insulators from the electrified track have been recovered from the station and can be seen at the London Transport Museum. Copyright London Regional Transport

Below: King William Street station was located almost under the Monument, Wren's Doric column to commemorate the Fire of London. The other underground station, also located in King William Street, was called Monument on the Metropolitan District Railway. Monument station remains open, but the original entrance, seen in this view, has long since been replaced. Copyright London Regional Transport

⑧ Underground Ghosts

There are few deep tube lines in London that have been built and then subsequently closed, yet there are several tube stations and surface buildings in London that are no longer in use. This is sometimes because new entrances have been constructed, such as at Hyde Park Corner, or at Euston. Elsewhere several stations have closed completely on lines that remain open and in a few cases both tube line and station have closed. Some losses of interest are outlined in this chapter.

Metropolitan Ghosts

In order to overcome fears about the ventilation of sulphurous fumes in subterranean stations when steam traction was used, John Fowler designed a fireless locomotive for the Metropolitan Railway. It became known as 'Fowler's Ghost', but in fact the engine used heated fire-bricks and was not a success.

Perhaps the ghost of Conan Doyle's Sherlock Holmes stalks a number of closed stations near Baker Street. As you head north, the train rattles past the derelict remains of three subterranean stations before emerging into daylight near Finchley Road. Lord's closed in November 1939 together with Marlborough

```
                              ✪ BULL & BUSH

         SOUTH KENTISH TOWN ✪
                                         ✪ YORK ROAD
    MARLBOROUGH ROAD ✪
                        LORD'S ✪  CITY ROAD ✪
                         ✪ UXBRIDGE ROAD
                    ✪ WOOD LANE          ✪ MUSEUM
          ✪ SOUTH ACTON          ✪ DOWN ST
             ✪                            ✪ ALDWYCH
       HAMMERSMITH    ✪ BROMPTON RD
       GROVE ROAD      KING WILLIAM STREET ✪
```

Below: St John's Wood Road station before rebuilding and renaming as St John's Wood in 1925. In June 1939 the station was again renamed as Lord's, but closed in November 1939 in order to relieve congestion on this busy section of line out of Baker Street. Copyright London Regional Transport

Road, while Swiss Cottage hung on until August of the following year. They were closed primarily to reduce congestion on this busy two-track section of Metropolitan Line when the new parallel Bakerloo Line opened and was able to offer alternative stations.

A Curse and a Lost City on the Central

The Central London Railway opened between Shepherd's Bush and Bank in July 1900. Museum station was also opened on that date, but closed in September 1933. This particular closure came in for some scrutiny at the time as the station served one of the key passenger generators on the line: the British Museum. Closure was attributed by one newspaper to an Egyptian mummy haunting the station from the museum above and rumours of a secret passage to the tube station were reported. Indeed a driver once reported a person covered in bandages on the line, but nothing was ever found. The reality was simply that nearby Holborn made a better interchange station with the Piccadilly Line. During World War 2, Museum station was used as an air-raid shelter and today its

tiled walls are still visible in the sinister darkness from the passing trains.

Although not in the deep tube, Wood Lane was opened by the Central London Railway in May 1908 to serve the Franco-British Exhibition, whose white-painted buildings led to it being called White City. The Exhibition closed in October 1908 and eventually the buildings were demolished, including the commodious footbridge that led to Wood Lane station. Freight (including milk) and passengers were handled at the station until its closure in 1947, when the nearby new White City station opened, allowing through working of the extended line. In 1998 parts of Wood Lane station still existed, although in a derelict condition, over 50 years after closure.

Below: Passengers wait at the British Museum station for trains on the Central London Railway. Note the passageways that lead onto the platform; perhaps one secretly lead to the Egyptian remains in the British Museum! Copyright London Regional Transport

Top Secret on the Piccadilly

Rationalisation of stations on the Piccadilly Line led to a number of closures, including Down Street station which was closed in May 1932. Being in the very heart of London it was used during World War 2 as secret wartime bunker for the Railway Executive Committee and War Cabinet. Ministers would travel with the tube driver and enter the converted station via a secret door at tube level. The station buildings remain. York Road opened in December 1906 and closed in September 1932. Leslie Green was the architect. The surface buildings here are still extant and used by businesses in a bleak part of the area north of King's Cross. Access is still available to the track. Finally, Brompton Road station closed in 1934 as it was considered too close to South Kensington.

Nonstop Northern

South Kentish Town opened in June 1907 and closed in June 1924, although before closure some trains passed through without stopping. Leslie Green was again the architect. The platforms have been removed leaving a black void, but the station itself remains at surface level and is in retail use as trains rattle past below. Another station where trains never stopped was at Bull and Bush, north of Hampstead. The station was

Above: A ghostly reminder of the past. A seat with the station name of Museum is to be found outside the London Transport Museum at Covent Garden. The museum opened in 1973 and the seat is viewed here in August 1997. Author

Below: The street-level entrance to the British Museum underground station is seen here, with a large arrow indicating the way to the nearby Piccadilly Line interchange station at Holborn. The closeness and convenience of Holborn as an interchange station was the real reason for the closure of the British Museum station. Copyright London Regional Transport

constructed at track level in 1907, but was so deep below the ground that it was decided not to use it. It was rumoured that the jollity from the Bull and Bush pub above could be heard on the unused platforms. Finally, City Road on the Angel extension did not reopen after reconstruction of the line in 1922 and is currently used as a store.

A Tea Run on the District

In June 1905 an electric service started operating from South Acton westward to Hounslow. However, in the following month, electric services also started to run east from Acton Town to Earl's Court. This latter service led to a change in the main traffic flows and the South Acton section of line became a shuttle service from Acton Town. Not forming part of the main route to the City, a one-car train maintained the service on the link until passenger closure in February 1959. The 2min journey time was so short that stories that tea could be made by the time the train ran up and down the line gave rise to the line being known as 'the tea run'.

Also of interest at South Acton, the North & South Western Junction Joint Railway provided the opportunity to travel, until 1916, to its terminus at Hammersmith & Chiswick. Freight ran on this branch line until 1965. By 1977 there were complaints that the acres of land at the Hammersmith terminus had not been redeveloped, but today the area and most of the branch have been built over.

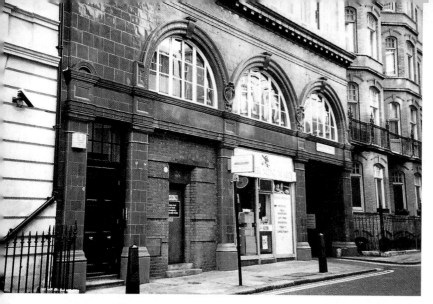

Below: At Hyde Park Corner the former station buildings have been converted into a restaurant, as this view taken in September 1997 shows. The maroon glazed blocks look as good as new and good use has been made of the large semicircular windows. Author

Below: York Road station opened in December 1906 and closed in September 1932. Viewed here in September 1997, the surface buildings were in commercial use, but emergency access to the tube below was still possible. Author

Above: The substantial South Kentish Town station which opened in 1907 and closed in June 1924, after a mere 17 years of use. In 1910 the Hampstead Line was absorbed by the London Electric Railway and a map on the right of the building shows London's underground electric railways.
Copyright London Regional Transport

Below: Former tube buildings at Euston, to the designs of Leslie Green. The single-storey buildings were built with the intention that accommodation could be added above. This underground station was located on the opposite side of Cardington Street from the main line station. Redevelopment of Euston and addition of the Victoria Line allowed all the tube lines to surface in the main line station concourse. The former underground station, shown here in September 1997, now houses electrical equipment. Author

Left: South Kentish Town station in September 1997: the street-level buildings were being used for retail purposes at this time. The distinctive architecture of Leslie Green and James Chapman remains apparent. Author

Centre left: London Transport modified two 'G' cars for single-man operation on the South Acton branch. Here one of the single electric units has arrived at the short platform at South Acton. The line, which opened in 1905, closed in February 1959. David Lawrence

Left: Map of the Acton Town to South Acton branch of the District Line in 1938. Crown copyright

⑨ To the Palace Gates

The opening of Alexandra Palace in May 1873 was seen as a great opportunity for the railways to carry the masses of people who wished to visit the new facilities. The Great Northern Railway constructed a line directly to the Palace itself. The Great Eastern Railway was determined to also benefit from this lucrative sports and entertainment complex and proposed a line from Seven Sisters to link into the Great Northern branch.

Such a proposal would have involved steep gradients at the palace end of the route and a more modest scheme for a 2¼-mile double-track line from Seven Sisters to the foot of the park complex at Palace Gates, was put forward. This was opened as far as Green Lanes, later renamed Noel Park, in January 1878 and to Palace Gates in October of the same year. The substantial Palace Gates station was constructed for through running. This allowed access to the locomotive shed and goods yard beyond, but it was perhaps also designed with the prospect of a closer link to Alexandra Palace in mind, as Palace Gates station was almost a mile from the palace itself.

Unlike its Great Northern counterpart, the line was not almost entirely dependent on Alexandra Palace itself for its patronage, and commuting developed. Trains ran to Liverpool Street and to North Woolwich, where a ferry and subway ran to Woolwich proper. Here, at one time, Woolwich Arsenal operated a network of lines and provided much employment.

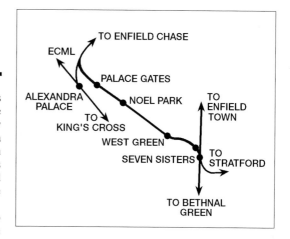

Below: A Thompson Class L1 2-6-4T, No 67729, leaves Lea Bridge on the 4.16pm North Woolwich to Palace Gates train on 1 June 1962. The locomotive was one of 100 built between 1946 and 1950. All were withdrawn by the end of 1962. L. Sandler

A considerable passenger service developed, with over 50 weekday departures from Palace Gates in 1910.

In 1930 the LNER provided some investment in the line, including a link at Palace Gates from the former Great Eastern branch to the Great Northern Hertford North branch, to facilitate stock movements. The link was fully signalled for through running in 1944 to provide greater route flexibility during World War 2.

In spite of some through running from Hertford and Enfield, the line operated principally as a branch. Through services to Liverpool Street ended in 1947. No

attempt at modernisation, or electrification was made. Tram, bus and the nearby tube station at Wood Green had all cut into the line's revenue. By 1955 departures from Palace Gates had been reduced to under a dozen, and by the time of closure this had been cut further.

The branch was one of the lines in the London area identified as already closed in the Beeching Report; its links via the Tottenham & Forest Gate Joint line to Barking and the Tottenham & Hampstead Joint line to Gospel Oak were also included for closure. As it turned out these former joint lines survived, but Palace Gates station was seen to be duplicated by Wood Green underground station, and the fact that there was also a nearby station on the ECML meant that the branch line was doomed. Passenger services ended in January 1963 and the whole route closed to freight in February 1965. Much of the line has since been built over, but there are some reminders of the branch, including a short section of embankment at Seven Sisters.

The second branch line that served Alexandra Palace was operated by the Great Northern Railway and ran right to the Palace itself. This line opened in May 1873, and although well used at first, was very closely related to the fortunes of the Palace, being forced to close a number of times when the Palace was

Below: A Tottenham Hale to Stratford DMU calls at the deserted and unkempt Lea Bridge on the day before the station's closure. The Cravens DMU was a nice example of what Stratford could do. The cab roof, painted white, became quite common in later days of the depot. Despite the headboard, the train stands at Lea Bridge on 4 July 1985, from Tottenham Hale, on the penultimate day of operation. C. Boocock

Right: Seven Sisters on 11 October 1958. On the left Class N7 0-6-2T No 69647 waits with the 12.2pm North Woolwich to Palace Gates train. On the right a Class N7, No 69686, is also seen with the 12.28pm Palace Gates to North Woolwich train. K. Cook

Below right: Class N7 0-6-2T at Seven Sisters Junction, with the Palace Gates branch diverging into the foreground, shortly before the closure of the branch. The signalbox remained in use in 1998. David Lawrence

out of action. The line was once proposed for electrification and integration into the tube system and some preparatory works were carried out before World War 2. However, after the war, priorities were changed and the branch closed to passengers in July 1954. A more comprehensive history of this line is contained in the *Lost Lines: Eastern* volume.

Left: At Seven Sisters only a short length of the original branch remains. This view of a decaying bridge on the remaining section of disused line was taken in January 1998. Author

Below: A deserted and almost rural-looking West Green station, with Class L1 2-6-4T No 67735 and a train for Palace Gates on 17 March 1962. The line closed to passengers in January of the following year. R. N. Joanes

Right: Palace Gates station, also known as Palace Gate (Wood Green) with Class L1 No 67724 about to push the empty stock of the 1.27pm Saturdays only arrival from North Woolwich into the carriage sidings. M. Schumann

Below right: Class L1 2-6-4T No 67724 propels the stock of the 12.40pm Saturdays only from North Woolwich into the sidings after running round at Palace Gates on 2 June 1962. G. King

Table 15

PALACE GATES (Wood Green), SOUTH TOTTENHAM, STRATFORD, VICTORIA DOCK and NORTH WOOLWICH—Third Class only

(Timetable showing two sets of Week Days / Suns. columns)

Left panel — HOUR

Miles	HOUR	a.m. / Week Days / p.m / am / Suns.
	Palace Gates A .. dep	58 26 40 . 31 . 36 . 52 16 37 31 54 33 U V . . .
1	Noel Park F.........	0 28 42 . 33 . 38 . 54 18 39 33 56 35 . . . .
1¼	West Green	3 31 45 . 36 . 41 . 67 21 42 36 59 38 . . . .
	Seven Sisters.. arr	5 33 48 . 39 . 43 . 59 23 44 38 1 40 . . . .
2¼	{ dep	6 34 55 . . 43 44 49 0 24 45 39 2 41 . 24 .
2½	South Tottenham	9 37 58 . . 47 52 3 27 48 42 5 44 . . .
4¼	Lea Bridge............	15 45 4 15 . 55 54 59 9 36 56 48 11 50 26 34 .
	Stratford (L.L.). arr	23 53 12 23 L 5 2 7 17 44 4 56 19 58 34 .
7¼	{ dep	27 54 18 26 . 8 19 45 6 1 21 0 36 . .
7¾	Stratford Market	29 56 20 28 . 7 10 21 47 8 3 23 2 38 . .
9	Canning Town	33 0 24 32 . 11 14 25 51 12 7 27 6 42 . .
10½	Custom House B	37 4 28 36 . 15 18 29 55 16 11 31 10 46 . .
11	Silvertown	40 7 31 39 . 18 21 32 58 19 14 34 13 49 . .
12¾	North Woolwich.. arr	43 10 34 42 . 21 24 35 1 22 17 37 16 52 . .

Right panel — HOUR

Miles	HOUR	a.m. / Week Days / p.m. / Suns.
1	North Woolwich..dep	30 25 58 0 24 46 8 51 4 . 44 18 34 49 8 38 38 P
1	Silvertown	33 28 1 3 27 49 6 54 7 . 47 21 37 52 11 41 41 Z
2	Custom House B......	36 31 4 6 30 52 9 57 10 . 50 24 40 55 14 44 44 .
3	Canning Town	40 35 8 20 34 56 13 13 14 . 54 28 44 59 18 48 48 .
4½	Stratford Market......	44 39 12 24 38 0 2 17 5 18 . 58 32 48 3 22 52 52 .
5	Stratford (L.L.). arr	46 41 14 26 40 2 19 7 20 . 0 34 50 5 24 54 54 .
	{ dep	47 42 15 27 42 4 20 8 25 L26 1 35 51 10 25 0 55 .
8	Lea Bridge............	56 51 24 36 51 13 29 17 34 44 10 44 0 19 34 9 4 8 56
10	South Tottenham	2 57 31 43 Y 19 39 23 40 . 16 50 6 K 40 16 10 .
10½	Seven Sisters.... arr	3 59 32 44 . 20 40 24 42 52 18 51 7 . 42 17 11 9 10
11	{ dep	4 5 33 45 . 21 41 25 48 . 23 52 8 . 48 18 12 .
11	West Green	7 8 36 48 . 24 44 28 51 . 26 55 11 . 51 21 15 .
12	Noel Park F.........	11 12 40 52 . 28 48 32 55 . 30 59 15 . 55 25 19 .
12¾	Palace Gates A....arr	14 15 43 55 . 31 51 35 58 . 33 2 18 . 58 28 22 .

Notes:

A Palace Gate (Wood Green)
B Custom House (Vic. Dock)
E or E Except Saturdays
F Noel Park and Wood Green
F Fridays only
H Saturdays only. Runs 23rd July to 10th Sept.
J Saturdays only. Runs 23rd July to 10th September. Through Train Enfield Town dep 7 24 am to Clacton-on-Sea arr 10 3 am (Tables 14 and 27)

K From or to Hertford (East) (Table 8)
L Mondays to Fridays, also runs Saturdays until 16th July and on 17th September
L Stratford (Main) Station
N Except Fridays and Saturdays
P Runs 10th July to 28th August
S or S Saturdays only
U From Tottenham (Table 8)
V Through Train Southend-on-Sea dep 11 5 am to Southend-on-Sea, arr 12 42 pm (Tables 14 and 18)

X Saturdays only. Commences 23rd July. Through Train Clacton-on-Sea, dep 2 50 pm to Enfield Town, arr 5 12 pm (Tables 27 and 14)
Y To Angel Road (Table 8)
Z Through Train Southend-on-Sea, dep 7 44 pm to Enfield Town, arr 9 30 pm (Tables 18 and 14)

Additional stopping trains on Week Days between Stratford (L.L.) and North Woolwich at 5 32, 5 48, 7 8, 7 48, 8 26, 9S7, 9 30, 10S21, 11S3, 11S21 and 11S41 am, 12S1, 12S22, 12F23, 12S45, 1F23, 1S44, 2F20, 2S51, 3F41, 3S51, 4F1, 4S51, 4S55, 5E11 5E31, 6F36 and 7E8 p.m., returning from North Woolwich to Stratford (L.L.) at 6 10, 6 57, 7 45, 8 8, 8 20, 8 35, 8 48, 9 7, 9 37, 10 36, 10S58, and 11S35 a.m., 12S2, 12F4, 1E2, 1S27, 1S49, 2E22, 2F52, 3S28, 4S28, 4E31, 4E58, 5S28, and 7E8 p.m.

For OTHER TRAINS between Lea Bridge and Stratford, see Table 8

Above: Services provided from Palace Gates in July 1955. Author's collection

Below: Unlike the GER Palace Gates branch, the GNR line reached the grounds of Alexandra Palace itself. This line closed in July 1954. The station at Alexandra Palace escaped demolition, together with a number of bridges on the line, such as this in the palace grounds and viewed here in August 1994. Author

10 Behind Closed Doors

There are considerably more than 100 lost stations on lines that remain open in the London area. They are located in all parts of the city and *prima facie* their reopening could represent a considerable reduction in traffic congestion. However, on closer examination of the reasons for closure, the reopening of many individual stations would probably not have any significant effect on London's traffic congestion.

Economics played a major part in the closures. Some stations were just too close to each other and savings could be made without significant loss of custom; the electric tram, the tube, buses and cars put paid to others; expensive renewals were another reason for closure and on top of all this came World War 2 damage. Operating difficulties resulted in the removal

of others, particularly where they were located on routes close to busy main line terminal stations, or where reconstruction was more easily achieved on a nearby new site.

Individual closures, which have occurred from early times, are too numerous to record in a single chapter, but some interesting examples are explored in this section. In order to save money on land costs, several of the closed stations had the majority of their facilities located under the viaduct on the line they served. Once closed and the surface platforms removed, some are surprisingly hard to distinguish.

Travelling out from Liverpool Street, nearby Bishopsgate Low Level closed in May 1916, although some of the platforms are still visible. Globe Road &

Right: Bishopsgate Low Level station, located just outside Liverpool Street. The platform remained in 1998, together with access to the nearby street. Although closed in May 1916, the platform has been retained for emergency use. Author

Below right: A cast-iron sign over the entrance to Globe Road & Devonshire station. The station opened in 1884 and closed in May 1916, again one of the earlier closures in the London area. This view shows the station area when it was being occupied by an engineering firm. David Lawrence

Devonshire station also closed in May 1916. Coborn Road for Old Ford closed in 1946 as part of the rationalisation for main line electrification. Platforms, supporting walls and entry stairs are still visible.

Running out of Fenchurch Street a number of former LTSR stations were duplicated by the District Line. Consequently, on the electrification of the Southend line in 1962, the main line side of stations at Bromley-by-Bow, West Ham, Manor Road, Plaistow, Upton Park and East Ham were closed.

On the approaches to St Pancras, the Midland Railway in 1916 closed stations either side of Kentish Town at Camden Road and Haverstock Hill, due mainly to tram competition. At Finchley Road the nearby tube led to the closure of the former Midland station in 1927. The Great Northern Railway closed Holloway station in 1915, the nearby Piccadilly Line being able to provide an alternative direct service to King's Cross.

The tube did not penetrate so extensively south of the river, but in fact there have been many main line station closures here. The wonderfully evocative name Spa Road, just outside London Bridge (from where London's first railway opened to Deptford in 1836) is one such example. A later station on the site dating from 1842 and closed in 1915 still retains its subways, while South Bermondsey, closed in 1928, retains its shabby street-level buildings.

Between Loughborough Junction and the Elephant and Castle, the tracks widen out to twice display dilapidated remains of Walworth Road and Camberwell New Road stations, both of which succumbed to the

Above right: The former GER Stratford Market station was rebuilt in 1892 and closed in June 1957. In the 1950s over 60 freight trains a day passed through the four tracks of the station. When viewed here, in September 1997, the station had been recently refurbished for use as offices. Trains still use the line through the station. Author

Right: Stratford main line station dates from 1839. It is not a lost station, but has been repeatedly altered over the years. A once-elegant door leads to derelict buildings, near Platform 10A. The door is viewed here in April 1998 and is a reminder of the former importance of the station. Author

electric tram in 1916. At Camberwell the nearby public house is still called The Station.

Travelling out from Victoria station, the SECR Grosvenor Road station buildings remain to the road, but the platforms have long since disappeared since final closure in 1911. Battersea Park Road platforms have also long gone since closure in 1916, together with those at East Brixton which closed much later in 1976. So effectively have the platforms been removed that at all three locations, at track level, you could hardly imagine that a station ever existed.

Travelling west, fewer stations on the former Western Region lines have closed. While differing policies between regions could be claimed, in reality the distribution of London stations on the Western was generally less profuse, particularly compared with some parts of the former South Eastern lines.

Wherever you travel around London there are, under many bridges and viaducts, entrances to stations that once bustled with activity. Most have been blocked up to prevent entry. Where once stylish stationmasters passed, you can only speculate what now might be found behind some of the closed doors.

Below left: One of the entrances at Holloway & Caledonian Road station on the ECML, viewed here in September 1997. The station closed in 1915, mainly as a result of competition from the nearby Piccadilly Line station. Author

Below centre: Grosvenor Road station opened in 1867 and was located almost at the end of the platforms of Victoria station. The SECR station, which closed in 1911, is viewed here from Grosvenor Road in September 1997. When Grosvenor Bridge was replaced in 1963, the opportunity was taken to provide an additional track in the area once occupied by the closed station's platforms. Author

Below right: South Bermondsey station was until 1869 called Rotherhithe. The LBSCR station closed in June 1928, but a new station was opened nearby. Most of the original station's facilities were located under the viaduct. The distinctive LBSCR-coloured brickwork to the window arches was still apparent when this view was taken in May 1998. Author

Above: Plaistow station, on the former London, Tilbury & Southend Railway. The derelict condition of buildings, seen here in April 1998, belies the adjoining platforms on the District Line which had recently been refurbished. The 'main line' side of the station, together with some others also served by the District Line, closed with the electrification of the Southend line in 1962. Author

11 Clearing Houses

Apart from stations the railways owned much other property in London. Foremost were the railway hotels and offices, but a range of other premises were once railway-owned. Amongst the more unusual railway property portfolios could be found a public house, The Blackfriar, near Blackfriars station, and false house fronts, for amenity purposes, at 23 and 24 Leinster Gardens, near Bayswater station.

Some hotels have been lost. The London Bridge Terminus Hotel, designed by H. Curry and opened in 1862, closed in 1893 and was used as offices until it was destroyed by bombs in 1940. The City Terminus Hotel opened in 1866 and was designed by E. M. Barry. It was renamed the Cannon Street Hotel in 1879. The hotel, which was similar in design to that at Charing Cross, although reduced by a floor, closed following Blitz damage in 1941. The Holborn Viaduct Hotel was opened by the LCDR in November 1877. It closed in 1917 and became offices, although the ground floor refreshment rooms remained until 1931. It was also demolished after Blitz fire damage in 1941.

The Euston Hotel opened in 1839 and was the first major railway hotel in the world. Much of the original classical design was by Philip Hardwick and it was built primarily for passengers using the London & Birmingham Railway. It was extended to 300 rooms by J. B. Stansby. Sadly this hotel, which survived World War 2, did not survive the 'Swinging Sixties' and it was demolished in 1963 to make room for the new Euston station.

Fortunately, a flavour of the splendour of the old railway companies can be gained by a visit to one of the former railway hotels that still remain in London, although none is now in railway ownership.

In 1854 the Great Western Railway Hotel opened at Paddington and is described in more detail in the *Lost Lines Western* volume. Rooms in which the GWR directors once met survived very much in their original condition, prior to closure of the hotel for refurbishment in 1998.

The Great Northern Hotel at King's Cross also opened in 1854 and was designed by Lewis Cubitt. It remains in use and is functional and modest in tone. Almost underneath the hotel runs the deserted 'Hotel Curve' line that once connected King's Cross main line station to the Widened Lines.

Below left: The former Euston Hotel's classical linking facade. Designed by J. B. Stansby, the extension complemented Hardwick's original design and increased accommodation at the hotel to 300 rooms, but it obscured views of the Doric Arch from the Euston Road. This splendid building, the first railway hotel in the world, was demolished in 1963. Ian Allan Library

Right: The Great Eastern Hotel's spiral staircase at Liverpool Street, dating from 1884 and viewed here in 1964. C. E. Barry and R. W. Edis were responsible for the completed hotel. Plans to demolish this highly attractive building were scrapped and the hotel underwent extensive renovation in 1998. Author

The Grosvenor Hotel at Victoria station was opened in 1861. The hefty design, by J. T. Knowles, provided a fine Roman staircase and the hotel was unique in its early use of concrete mouldings to simulate stone. A direct entrance to the station still exists.

The Charing Cross Hotel was opened in 1864 by the South Eastern Railway in the very centre of London. The hotel was damaged in World War 2, but the upper two storeys were repaired and rebuilt in a modern style and the hotel remains open.

The Midland Grand Hotel was designed by Sir George Gilbert Scott and opened in May 1873. Used as offices and renamed St Pancras Chambers on closure in April 1935, it is one of London's greatest landmarks. The Gothic splendour of the interior, with its grand intertwining double staircase, magnificent restaurant and smoking room, is to be restored as a luxury hotel.

The Great Eastern Hotel at Liverpool Street was designed by C. E. Barry, and opened in May 1884. It was extended in 1899 to the design of R. W. Edis. Most of the hotel, including the domed dining room and spiral staircase, survived the redevelopment of the station. In 1998 the hotel was closed for refurbishment.

The last railway hotel built in London was opened by the Great Central Railway in 1899, at Marylebone. The huge hotel closed in 1939, but after being utilised as offices the building is again in use as a hotel. Although no longer called the Great Central Hotel much of the original sumptuous character remains. In 1998 the most expensive daily rate for rooms exceeded £1,000.

In contrast to the Great Central Hotel, the modest Gallions Hotel in Docklands was owned by the London & St Katharine Dock Co and was completed in 1883 to designs by Vigers and Wagstaff. The hotel is a listed building and remains standing, but it was last used in 1972 and is currently disused.

Many small administrative railway buildings have been demolished in London. However, the substantial Harwich House, dating from 1890 and used by the Great Eastern Railway, was demolished with the reconstruction of Liverpool Street station. At Paddington, the decline in freight led to the demolition of a substantial office block in Bishop's Bridge Road.

Former railway offices of interest that remain are at Eversholt House near Euston station. Originally the headquarters of the LMS, the building was once adorned with huge LMS initials. Also in Eversholt Street is Carriage Row, which was designed by Hardwick. This was the railway 'clearing house' where railway companies settled their ticket and financial arrangements. Galleries were provided for supervisors to keep an eye on the 2,500 clerks once employed below. The building remains and the galleries were retained in a refurbishment. Near Paddington former offices of the GWR are still distinguished by a huge GWR concrete symbol, although it is now many years since they were in railway use. Other railway companies also had offices in London, ranging from the offices of the North Eastern Railway in Cowley Street to the Canadian Pacific Railway buildings in Trafalgar Square.

Left: Part of the grand staircase in the former Midland Grand Hotel at St Pancras, designed by Sir George Gilbert Scott, with décor dating from 1901. The staircase is viewed here after closure of the hotel in 1935 and when the building was used as offices known as St Pancras Chambers. British Railways

Below: Cannon Street station hotel was also designed by E. M. Barry in a similar fashion to that at Charing Cross. The hotel at Cannon Street had 84 bedrooms, but it was not a success and was converted to offices in the 1930s. The building was damaged to such an extent by air-raids in World War 2 that it had to be demolished. Author's collection

GREAT WESTERN ROYAL
─ HOTEL ─

Right: Charing Cross station with the French Tricolour flying over the hotel on 14 July 1942, Bastille Day. The hotel was designed by E. M. Barry and opened in 1864. The SR directors always dined here before board meetings. The hotel was badly damaged in World War 2 and the upper floors were subsequently rebuilt to a more modern style.
Southern Railway

Below: Paddington, with the front elevation of the goods office in Bishop's Bridge Road, on 25 July 1946. The offices opened in 1906 and about 5,000 staff were once employed at the goods depot, before decline began in the 1950s. The offices were demolished after closure of the depot, see view on page 18. GWR Photographic Department

12 A Loop to a Lost Empire

History has seen the rise and fall of many empires. The British Empire, at one time or another, held sway over a quarter of the world's land mass and London was its centre. The Empire was at its fullest extent in 1919, and Wembley Stadium was one of many buildings erected in the 1920s in connection with the British Empire Exhibition which ran from 1924-5. In 1924 the LNER opened Wembley Exhibition station specifically for the Empire Exhibition.

The huge Palace of Engineering at the exhibition, was linked to a new loop line by a series of sidings. The exhibits included a number of the latest railway developments ranging from Sentinel railcars to the Gresley Pacific locomotive *Flying Scotsman*. This latter locomotive was billed by the LNER as the most powerful passenger engine in Great Britain. This statement was challenged by the GWR, which on their adjoining stand exhibited the smaller, but higher boiler-pressured *Caerphilly Castle*.

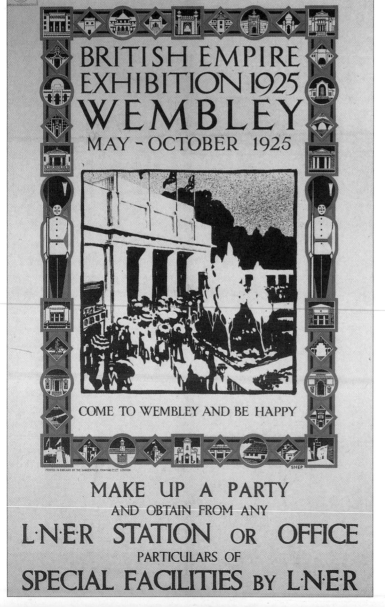

Left: A LNER poster extolling the delights of the Wembley Exhibition. Science & Society Picture Library

Right: Crowds depart from a train at Wembley Stadium station on 24 April 1948. On this occasion Manchester United and Blackpool were playing the FA Cup Final at Wembley. British Railways

Below right: A view of Wembley Stadium station from the west end on 24 April 1948, showing the distinctive concrete design. The station was known as Wembley Exhibition until 1928. The single platform on the loop line was traversed in a clockwise direction. British Railways

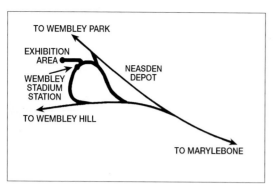

To WEMBLEY PARK

EXHIBITION AREA

WEMBLEY STADIUM STATION

NEASDEN DEPOT

TO WEMBLEY HILL

TO MARYLEBONE

Wembley Exhibition station was built in concrete to a 1920s modern 'art deco' style to reflect the design of other buildings erected for the exhibition. It had a single platform capable of holding eight coaches and was located on a 1-mile loop that diverged from the Northolt line just west of Neasden. The loop together with the line to Marylebone was equipped with state-of-the-art three-aspect electric colour-light signalling, the first use of such signalling on a main line. The loop also enabled services to run out and back to Marylebone without the need for reversal.

The station was extensively used for the exhibition and again, after a change in name to Wembley Stadium, in 1948 when the Olympic Games used Wembley Stadium. It was also used for other events at Wembley, such as football Cup Finals. These events could generate 100,000 spectators and most would use public transport. To meet this level of demand at peak times trains would leave Marylebone every 8min for the 12min trip to the Stadium station. This would require the services of eight trains and nine locomotives. The line would not be used when events were not in progress, apart from turning locomotives.

The line served a useful purpose in carrying passengers to special events, but the service did not appear in timetables by virtue of the fact that regular daily services were not provided. As such this is probably why it did not appear in the Beeching Report for closure. Nevertheless, the loop had a brief history of just over 50 years. The last train ran to the station in May 1968, although official closure was not until September of the following year.

Today, one of the concrete bridges on the route is still visible, but in the 30 years or so since closure there has been much rebuilding over the line and the route is hardly discernible. Just as the station has gone, so has the British Empire. India became independent in 1947 and from 1956, one by one, the states of Africa achieved their freedom. In 1997 Hong Kong passed from British rule.

Below left: Demolition in progress at Wembley Stadium station on 6 April 1974, after formal closure of the line in 1969. N. Whitburn

Right: The remains of a concrete bridge over the Wembley loop line in September 1997. Although parts of the loop are still visible, in general, redevelopment has resulted in almost its complete disappearance from the area. Author

Below: Remains of one of the buildings used for the Empire Exhibition in 1924-5, giving an impression of the general style used. The derelict building is seen here in September 1997. Author

13 Docklands

London was a port long before it became a great city; since early times it has been the upper limit for sea-going vessels. The section of Thames between Tower Bridge and London Bridge is known as the Pool of London and was the original port area. Over the centuries, the port has developed to reflect changes in trading patterns and transport. As steam replaced sail, the size of ships expanded and the volume of trade grew, all increasing the need for new docks further downriver. Dock building was facilitated by the soft soil and marshes that lined the Thames.

Not all the original docks were rail-served, but the India and Millwall Docks were. The railways were also behind the building of the Royal Docks. The Victoria Dock, designed for steamships, was opened in 1855, Albert Dock opened in 1880 and King George V Dock opened in 1921, completing the 'Royals' and the series of rail-served docklands that developed on the Thames.

As competition from other ports intensified, a Royal Commission was set up to examine the operation of London's docklands. As a result all the individual dock companies were joined together in 1909 as the Port of London Authority. The PLA also took over the internal railway systems and at its height ran over 140 miles of line.

The network of dockland lines fed into a number of freight depots; the Midland, Great Western, Great Northern, Great Eastern, London & North Western and North London railways all had depots in the area from which freight was dispatched. However, because a

fleet of over 8,000 lighters were able to operate in the dockland area, the great marshalling yards that are often associated with docklands elsewhere did not develop in London.

Apart from freight, a number of passenger services also ran in the docklands area, but some were early candidates for closure. The tram and motorbus put an end to the Blackwall and North Greenwich passenger services in 1926. The passenger services from Custom House to Beckton, where the gasworks was the largest in the world, closed in September 1940 together with services on the PLA spur to Gallions. The Broad Street to Poplar service came to an end in 1944, having suffered considerable damage during World War 2.

After World War 2 the docks saw a period of continual contraction. As the size of ships increased and containerisation developed, the upper docks declined in particular, together with rail as the main form of freight transport. East India Docks closed in 1967 and Surrey Docks in 1970. The Royals hung on until closure in 1981, although rail services ended in 1970.

Damage to the area during World War 2, followed later by extensive redevelopment, has resulted in the loss of much of the original railway infrastructure. However, a number of bridges and viaducts has remain. At North Woolwich, the once near-derelict station has become a railway museum. Today, Docklands is transformed. The Docklands Light Railway was opened in July 1987 and a network of lines uses many general alignments of formerly closed railway.

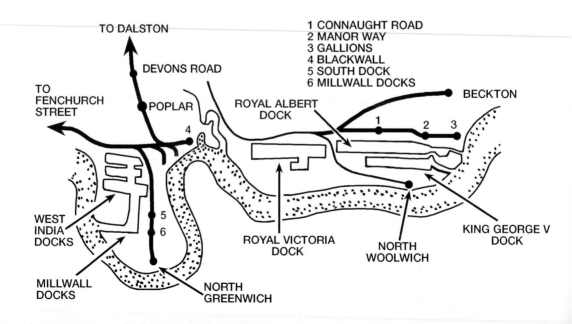

Passenger services run once again to Poplar, North Greenwich (now called Island Gardens), Blackwall, Gallions and Beckton.

Further down the Thames is the Port of Tilbury. The railway reached the town in 1854 and Tilbury Docks opened in 1886. Part of the docks remains rail- served. Passengers originally used Tilbury Riverside station as a downriver alternative to London and as a ferry crossing to Gravesend. A substantial station was opened in 1930, but use declined and Riverside station was closed in 1992, and in 1998 was in a derelict state.

Above: The Pool of London at Tower Pier. The Ich Dien, a passenger-carrying tug, is seen here with Tower Bridge in the background. The view shows how busy the upper river and Pool of London once were. Although freight traffic has largely disappeared, pleasure trips such as this remain as popular as ever.
C. R. L. Coles

Right: Services on the Millwall Extension Railway were operated for four decades by a number of Manning Wardle 2-4-0Ts of the Millwall Dock Company. Here No 6 poses at a dockland station with staff and a train of two GER carriages. Real Photographs

Left: A photograph of a Royal Albert Dock 2-4-0T and train for Custom House waiting at Gallions station, prior to the working of the line by the GER in 1896. The PLA line to Gallions closed to passenger traffic after World War 2 air-raid damage in September 1940. Ian Allan Library

Above: A PLA Hudswell Clarke 0-4-0ST, No 47, at work in Millwall Dock, crossing the South Dock/Millwall Dock swing bridge. The view was taken in March 1960 when a party of enthusiasts visited the loco shed at Millwall. The locomotive was withdrawn from service the following year. C. R. L. Coles

Left: PLA No 80, an 'Austerity' 0-6-0ST, simmers at Custom House on 12 October 1957. The locomotive was taken into PLA stock after an earlier World War 2 loan from the Ministry of Defence. T. Rowe

Above: South Quay looking north. When this view was taken, on 28 September 1983, the commercial use of the upper docks was almost at an end. South Quay was subsequently bridged by the Docklands Light Railway and much of the dock itself is now used for leisure activity. J. Glover

Below: An 0-4-0ST, PLA No 89, viewed here on 26 October 1957 at Millwall on the once extensive railway network that served the docks. The locomotive was one of the last built for the PLA and was withdrawn from service in 1961. T. Rowe

Above: Silvertown station on 13 May 1985, the first day of EMU working on a line that remains open. EMU 2-EPB No 6315 is seen pausing in the station at about midday. The line to the left of the view is a spur that served dockland factories and was once the original route to North Woolwich. Ian Allan Library

Above right: Silvertown in September 1997 with the Silvertown Tramway, the original route to North Woolwich, much overgrown. The view is unique, in that the level crossing was one of the few to remain so close to central London. Author

Centre right: The Gallions Hotel in April 1998. The rural surroundings belie the fact that, when open, the hotel had views of dockland warehousing and Beckton Gasworks. Passenger liners used the nearby pier, but in later years it was alleged that the dockland hotel had a bit of a colourful reputation. Author

Right: Downstream at Tilbury was Riverside station. The substantial neo-Georgian passenger facility, designed by Sir Edwin Cooper, was unused when this view was taken in December 1997. Constructed in the late 1920s, it was estimated that 1,000 vessels used this section of the Thames each day at that time. Riverside station, after years of declining passenger usage, closed in 1992. Author

14 Greenwich Deadlines

The meridian line of zero passes through Greenwich, and Greenwich Mean Time was to provide the international basis for all the world's railway timetables. The first railway to Greenwich was the London & Greenwich Railway which ran from Spa Road, near London Bridge, and reached Greenwich by December 1838. The line was built on a viaduct of 878 arches, with the original notion that homes could be provided under the arches. The housing idea was not a success, but the railway was and remains in use, unlike a number of later lines that were built to serve the Greenwich area.

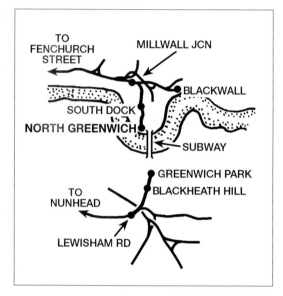

North Greenwich

The route to North Greenwich developed as part of a network of lines that served the docks to the north of Greenwich Reach, on the Isle of Dogs. The London & Blackwall Railway opened a line from Blackwall to Minories in July 1840, which was extended to Fenchurch Street the following year. The company was the first to operate steamships and the line enabled passengers to arrive in central London more swiftly than if they had continued their trip from Gravesend to the Pool of London entirely by river.

From this original route a 1½-mile single line ran from Millwall Junction to North Greenwich. Known as the Millwall Extension Railway it opened throughout by July 1872. The line was leased to the Great Eastern Railway and an intensive passenger service developed between Fenchurch Street and the North Greenwich terminus, at Cubitt Town, which was located on the opposite river bank to Greenwich proper. Connection to Greenwich itself was at first by ferry; subsequently, however, a foot subway under the Thames was opened by the London County Council in 1902.

Below left: Stepney East with an EMU Class 302, No 312, approaching the station with a down train. In the foreground is the former Limehouse line to North Greenwich. Although disused when this view was taken on 27 September 1983, part of the route was subsequently reused by the Docklands Light Railway.
J. Glover

Above: Another view of the former route to North Greenwich, on 27 September 1983, which was to become part of a new route near Island Gardens on the DLR. A later DLR extension under the river to Greenwich proper will result in the reclosure of this viaduct. J. Glover

Right: The former GER North Greenwich station, in Fury Street, closed to passenger services in May 1926. The remaining part of the station is viewed here in 1964, prior to demolition. A new station on the Jubilee Line extension revives the North Greenwich name. L. Sandler

Passenger services gradually declined and this line was one of the few in London that closed with the General Strike in May 1926. After this, the southern section from the dock area to North Greenwich was abandoned, but freight continued on the northern part of the route which was realigned in 1928 to take account of dock extensions. By the early 1960s freight traffic was infrequent and closure came in 1966, although some traffic continued to run on a short northern spur from the former NLR line to Poplar Docks until 1974, and to a nearby scrap merchant until 1981. As it turned out, even this was not to be the end of rail services in the area. Part of the route was subsequently reopened in 1987 as the Docklands Light Railway. However, an extension under the river to Greenwich itself will result in the reclosure of part of the original high-level line between Mudchute and Island Gardens.

Greenwich Park

The line to Greenwich Park was opened by the London, Chatham & Dover Railway. It ran from Nunhead as far as Blackheath Hill by September 1871 and after concerns were resolved with the Greenwich Observatory, the line reached Greenwich by October 1888. The station was renamed Greenwich Park in 1900, to distinguish it from the original Greenwich station.

Although a frequent service was provided to Victoria, the branch had a surprisingly short passenger life. Greenwich had declined in importance: the route was less direct than the original line that ran into Charing Cross and trams had taken much of the inner suburban traffic. Receipts on the line fell alarmingly and as a World War 1 economy measure the branch, eastwards from Nunhead, closed in January 1917; although freight was retained from Nunhead to a coal depot at Brockley Lane.

In 1929 the Southern Railway reopened a mile of the former branch from Brockley Lane to beyond Lewisham Road, where connections were made to the Mid-Kent line. These new links allowed the Nunhead to Lewisham part of the branch to be used as an alternative link to the City.

On a foggy December evening in 1957 the Lewisham end of the reopened line was the scene of London's second-worst railway accident. A Bulleid Pacific smashed into the rear of an electric train that was halted on the Mid-Kent line under the bridge on the reopened branch line. The smash led to the collapse of the 350-ton overbridge onto the wreckage below. A train on the branch, about to cross over the collapsed bridge, managed to stop. Nevertheless 90 passengers were killed in the carnage below.

The section from Lewisham to Nunhead remains open, but the remaining section of the branch, via Blackheath Hill to Greenwich Park, was abandoned in 1929 and the track removed. Today most of the route has been built over, but some traces of the old line are still evident.

Above: A pedestrian tunnel under the River Thames links North Greenwich to Greenwich proper. Part has been strengthened, as can be seen in this view taken in May 1998. The resulting section of tunnel looks strikingly similar to the Tower Subway. Author

Left: Lewisham Road station on the remaining open section of the former Greenwich Park branch. The station opened in September 1871 and closed in January 1917. Some of the platform facilities still remain, although they had not been used for over 80 years when this view was taken in April 1998. Author

Above: It is clear from this view, taken in April 1998, that where the remaining line diverges to the right and to Lewisham, the original branch alignment once continued straight on towards Greenwich Park. Author

Left: Most of the Greenwich Park branch that remained closed after 1929 has been built over, but some sections remain. This overgrown embankment can be found near Lewisham Road. Just near this tranquil scene, a section of embankment was being removed for development when this view was taken in April 1998. Author

Below: The Brookmill Nature Reserve uses part of the closed Greenwich Park branch. An old covered railvan is appropriately used as a store and is seen here in April 1998. Author

The North London Railway, as it was called from 1853, was part of an ambitious scheme to link the Thames to north London and Birmingham. The first section to open, in September 1850, ran from Bow Junction to Islington. The route was extended to Hampstead Road (the now closed Primrose Hill station) in June 1851. The following year the line from Poplar to Bow was opened. At the same time freight services started operation and the link to the West India Docks allowed coal to be brought in by sea and delivered to the north London suburbs. By 1909 the NLR had administratively become part of the LNWR.

Broad Street

Traffic grew on the line and it was decided to run directly into the City from Dalston. The route into the City was heavily engineered and terminated at Broad Street (see *Lost Lines: LMR*). Passenger services over the 2-mile link were operating from November 1865 and freight ran to a two-tier terminal at Broad Street from May 1868. Services from Broad Street were heavily used at first and additional tracks were soon added. Such was the early success of the link that it became known as the 'Happy Afterthought'.

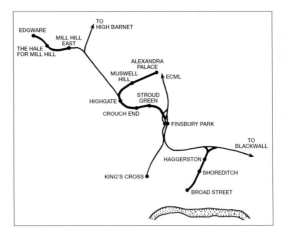

Below: In the 1900s about 40,000 passengers a day used Broad Street station during the morning peak. The busy approach to the station, seen here in LNWR days, is almost unrecognisable from its final years, when dereliction and weeds covered much of this area. Bucknall Collection

Above: The hugely cluttered entrance to Broad Street station in 1925, with a plethora of railway infrastructure and activity; a far cry from the last years of use of the line. Ian Allan Library

Below: Commuters pile off an early morning arrival hauled by a Brush Type 2 at Broad Street c1960. By this time only about 6,000 passengers used the station in the morning peak. British Railways

Above: A Class 501 EMU at Broad Street station on 14 February 1983. The roof had been hacked back after damage during World War 2 and half of the platforms are already disused and overgrown. J. Tickner

Left: A general view of Broad Street station in June 1984, before final demolition commenced. The original elegant Lombardic style was the work of William Baker. The street-level entrance can be seen to the left of the view. This 1913 addition, in a non-matching Portland stone, did nothing to improve the overall attractiveness of the station. M. J. Stretton

Above: A Class 501 EMU pauses at Dalston with a train for Broad Street, on 15 March 1967, just before the stock's repainting into blue livery. The station opened in November 1865 and closed in June 1986. Ian Allan Library

The effect of the tram and motorbus on the North London inner suburban services, that were the last in London to use wooden seats, was devastating and passenger numbers declined alarmingly after 1900. Some of the routes were electrified between 1916 and 1922 and this helped reverse the loss of passengers, but decline continued when the LMS took over in 1923. The passenger service from Dalston Junction to Poplar was ended in May 1944 and demolition of the line's stations, many of which were wrecked by the Blitz, commenced in 1947.

A section of what became well known as the North London Line, from Camden to Richmond, was proposed for passenger closure in the Beeching report. The Broad Street to Watford services were also proposed to be modified. However, the North London route to Richmond was reprieved in 1965.

The 'Happy Afterthought' was less fortunate. Broad Street was allowed to become the most derelict of all London's terminal stations and services to the site ended in June 1986. Much of the closed route still remains intact. At Dalston Junction, where connections both to the east and west were provided, the distinctive North London station architecture can still be found on a retaining wall. The line from Dalston to Broad Street was built largely on viaduct and the former four tracks still cut a fine swathe through this part of north London. There is little remaining of the two intermediate stations at Shoreditch and Haggerston, as they were damaged in the Blitz of World War 2 and closed to rail services in 1940. At the southern extremity, the viaduct suddenly ends at the new Broadgate development which covers the site of the former Broad Street station. Apart from Broadgate, there has been no serious blockage of this route and plans have been put forward to include the route as a northern extension of the East London Line.

Bow Works

Bow Works was established in 1863 and the NLR built its own highly distinctive 4-4-0 tank locomotives

Left: The track at Dalston is currently overgrown, as this view taken in September 1997 shows. The former Dalston station area itself is used for the storage of scrap cars. To the street level a small section of wall remains, with its distinctive North London architecture. Author

Below: LMR Class 501 EMU passing Western Junction with the 13.14 Broad Street to Richmond service on 16 May 1979. Western Junction was located at the northwest end of the spur that ran from the North London Line to Broad Street. In April 1998 the signalbox seen in this view still survived. L. Bertram

here. In its heyday over 30 acres of site straddled the North London line at Bow. The area was heavily blitzed in World War 2. In the end only wagons were repaired, but all work did not end at Bow Works until the mid-1960s. Today the site has been redeveloped. A former NLR 4-4-0 tank engine was selected for preservation by the LMS in 1929, but was regrettably scrapped. Other remains include NLR 0-6-0 tank locomotive No 116 which is preserved on the Bluebell Railway. Two original closely coupled four-wheel coaches are also retired on a remote steam line in Jersey, a location far removed from their original London environment.

Northern Heights

The use of other lines allowed trains from Broad Street to run to numerous north London destinations. Of particular interest were services over the GNR lines via Crouch End to Alexandra Palace, High Barnet and Edgware. The problems of sufficient capacity and financial expediency of the 1930s were amongst the reasons that led the LNER to agree to transfer these former GNR lines to London Transport for integration into the underground system. Unfortunately, as it turned out, World War 2 intervened to thwart some of the plans. Even so, by 1940 tube trains of the Northern Line were running to High Barnet, and the Edgware branch, which had closed in September 1939, had a section from Finchley to Mill Hill East reopened as part of the Northern Line in May 1941.

In the austere years that followed World War 2, it was decided not to proceed with electrification of the remaining lines to Edgware and to Alexandra Palace. The branch to Alexandra Palace and the link, via Crouch End, to Finsbury Park closed to passengers in July 1954. Freight remained to Edgware until June 1964, and over the Crouch End route to Finsbury Park until October 1970.

Above: The route from Broad Street to Dalston was built largely on viaduct. This large lattice-girder bridge over Kingsland Road, viewed here in September 1997, gives the impression that the line could still be open. Author

Below: The line to the north of Broad Street passed over the Regent's Canal. The bridge remains, but the decking had been removed when this view was taken in August 1997. Author

Left: The impressive Bow station, in distinctive North London style. Completed in 1870, the horse-drawn road vehicles would indicate that this view was taken in early LMS days. Damage during World War 2 resulted in the station's closure in May 1944 and subsequent demolition. Ian Allan Library

Below left: The North London Railway erecting shop at Bow on 7 June 1898, with the distinctive 4-4-0Ts Nos 44, 75 and 77 in view. Today, the site of the works has long been lost under housing development. Bucknall Collection

Right: The abandoned stairs to Highgate tube station, from the closed LNER high-level station, seen here in August 1994. Author's collection

Below: Services from Broad Street ran to many destinations. Here a North London train is seen leaving Crouch End on its way to Muswell Hill, c1900, travelling on a Great Northern section of line, from Finsbury Park to Highgate. Plans to make this route part of the Northern Line were abandoned after World War 2. Crouch End station closed to passengers in July 1954 and to all remaining freight traffic in 1970. Bucknall Collection

Above: Highgate station was rebuilt by the LNER. The station provided interchange with the new Northern Line tube station below. The former LNER station was closed in July 1954 and is viewed here in August 1994.
Author's collection

Below: Edgware was at the end of a former GNR branch line that at one time was proposed to provide a second LT Northern Line link to the area. Unfortunately, the tube never ran beyond Mill Hill East. The remaining section of branch closed to passengers in September 1939 and for freight in June 1964. This view shows a special trip over the line at Edgware, behind a Gresley Class N2 0-6-2T, in the late 1950s. David Lawrence

Above: The branch line to Alexandra Palace had track-side cables and supports laid in preparation for electrification. They were never put to use and the line closed in 1954. However, much of the electrical equipment still remains along the closed branch, as this view taken in August 1994, near Alexandra Palace, shows. Author

16 **South London Links**

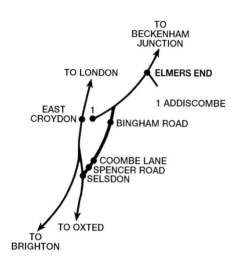

TO
BECKENHAM
JUNCTION

TO LONDON   ELMERS END

1 ADDISCOMBE

EAST   1
CROYDON   BINGHAM ROAD

COOMBE LANE
SPENCER ROAD
SELSDON

TO OXTED
TO
BRIGHTON

The Turn of the Tram

In April 1864 the South Eastern Railway opened a 3¼-mile link from New Beckenham to Croydon Addiscombe Road. After indecision as to its name (both Croydon Addiscombe and Addiscombe Croydon being used), the station finally became known as Addiscombe from 1925. Trains from London divided at New Beckenham, one portion running to Beckenham Junction, the other to Addiscombe. Housing was built in what was originally a rural area and the original station was replaced in 1899. Considerable traffic developed and this was boosted by electrification in 1926.

Freight ended in June 1968, but there was never any intention to close the line itself. Yet the 2-mile Elmers End to Addiscombe section closed quite recently and a special last train ran on 31 May 1997. Closure was because the area is served by the Croydon Tramlink and a northern part of the branch alignment is included in the new tram network.

A Lost Link Line

The 2½-mile link between Woodside and Selsdon Road was jointly owned by the LBSCR and the South Eastern Railway and opened in August 1885 as part of the Croydon & Oxted Joint Scheme. The line cut

Below: Addiscombe station with EMU 2-EPB units Nos 5753 and 5762 in the platforms on 5 June 1969. This was an attractive little terminus that my diary noted in 1974 as looking a little like the terminus at Felixstowe! J. Scrace

through a surprisingly hilly area and a tunnel and high bridges were required on the route. A shuttle service from New Beckenham ran over the line which was worked by the South Eastern Railway.

Spencer Road Halt was the first casualty and closed in September 1906. However, the entire Selsdon Road to Woodside line was closed during World War 1. The line was electrified and reopened by the SR in 1935, together with stations at Bingham Road and Coombe Lane, which became Coombe Road. Reflecting suburban growth in the area, on reopening Selsdon Road became known simply as Selsdon.

Services were again reduced during World War 2 and a decline set in. In 1949 off-peak through services to London were withdrawn. In 1959 services became peak hour only and Oxted services ceased to call at Selsdon. In 1963 the line was identified in the Beeching Report for closure. However, the local Member of Parliament, Ernest Marples, as the then Transport Minister, managed to prevent the closure of this line in his constituency. Services were cut back in 1967 and those remaining were reduced again during 1983, being withdrawn completely in May of that year.

Today at Coombe Road, the bridge over the road of that name has been demolished, together with the station. A similar situation applies at Bingham Road, where bridges have been demolished and where little of the station remains. At Selsdon the station has also

been closed, which is perhaps a pity as it is capable of being served by the Oxted line. The freight depot at this station still had its rail tracks remaining in 1997, but was heavily overgrown. The electric lights provided for the depot were in contrast to the once gas-lit station platforms. On its closure in 1983, Selsdon was the last remaining gas-lit station in south London. A section of the Croydon Tramlink uses the disused railway from Woodside as far as Coombe Road.

Southern Heights

A number of destinations in south London could once be found in a railway-theme restaurant at Hollywood in the USA. This establishment purchased the former manually operated destination board from Waterloo station and a mass of Southern Railway equipment. Unfortunately, the restaurant, together with a number of southern destinations, are no more.

In 1928 a Light Railway Order was obtained for the construction of the Southern Heights Light Railway, a line that, if built, would have connected Orpington to the Woodside to Selsdon link. The Southern Railway even showed the proposed light railway on their maps. The line was promoted by Colonel H. Stephens, but after his death the momentum and finance for the route drifted away and it was never constructed.

A short former LSWR and LBSCR Joint Railway loop line opened in 1868 and ran from Tooting to Merton Park. Passenger services ran to the one

Above left: EMU Class 416/2 2-EPB unit No 6277 enters Addiscombe with the 15.54 service from Elmers End, on Saturday 4 August 1990. At this time the station was unique as being the only remaining semaphore-signalling installation in the Southern Region's London suburban area.
Ian Allan Library

Above: Addiscombe station in September 1997, after closure of the line to Woodside in May of that year. Part of the former rail route is used for the Croydon Tramlink. The reintroduction of trams in Croydon will be the first time they have been seen in London since 1952. Author

Right: The line between Coombe Road and Selsdon Road involved several engineering structures, including a tunnel and bridges such as this over Croham Road, which was pictured here in September 1997. Author

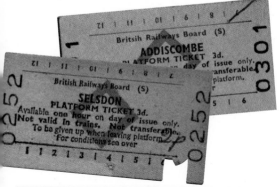

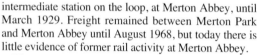

intermediate station on the loop, at Merton Abbey, until March 1929. Freight remained between Merton Park and Merton Abbey until August 1968, but today there is little evidence of former rail activity at Merton Abbey.

There were once two lines to Crystal Palace. That of the SECR, which ran to Crystal Palace High Level and closed in September 1954, is covered in more detail in *Lost Lines: Southern*. Crystal Palace itself burnt down in 1936 and little remains. The High Level station was also demolished after closure. Nevertheless one of the great railway treasures of London remains. This is the subway under Crystal Palace Parade. Built in 1865 by Italian crypt builders in red and white bricks, the wonderful subway is occasionally made available for public inspection in conjunction with tours of the former Crystal Palace site.

Above far left: The remains of Bingham Road station in September 1997. Closed in September 1906 as Bingham Road Halt, the station reopened in September 1935 as Bingham Road. In 1956 a return third-class fare from the station to London Bridge cost 3s 6d (17.5p). The station finally closed in 1983. Author

Above left: The line south of Bingham Road station once passed under Addiscombe Road, via a substantial bridge. When this view was taken, in September 1997, it was still possible to see the remains of porcelain insulators and other equipment associated with the electrification of the closed line. The Croydon Tramlink uses the railway formation at this point. Author

Left: Coombe Road on 4 August 1978. The station is deserted as an EMU 2-EPB No 5770 calls at the grass-covered down platform. This view is looking north towards the tunnel. Almost all trace of the station has been obliterated. The Croydon Tramlink uses the old railway formation as far as this station. J. Glover

Above: A rundown Selsdon station on 21 October 1962. The station was originally opened in 1885 and called Selsdon Road. It was partially closed in 1917, although an occasional Oxted train used the platforms. The station reopened as Selsdon in 1935 when the line was electrified. The station's platforms were gas-lit up until closure in 1983, the last so illuminated in the south London area. L. Sandler

Right: The only significant remains of Crystal Palace High Level station is a subway under the adjoining Crystal Palace Parade. This view of the substantial entrance, to a wonderful Italian crypt-style subway, is seen here in May 1995. Author

17 Secret Services and Circles

In 1840 the West London Railway opened a 2½-mile line from Willesden to the basin of the former Kensington Canal at Kensington. At this time the area was rural and traffic was sparse. However, the West London Extension, a 3-mile southerly link to Clapham Junction, led to the development of this cross-London route. The West London Line, as it became known, remains but much of its original infrastructure has been lost, including all but one of the stations, all the general freight yards and many of its connecting lines.

Kensington station was rebuilt in 1868 to a capacious LNWR style and was renamed Addison Road. The following year the LSWR opened a route from Addison Road, via Shepherd's Bush, to Hammersmith Grove Road, which allowed services to run directly to Richmond. By the early 1900s over 4 million passengers a year used Addison Road. In addition to through expresses, there were local services to all parts of London. The District Railway provided electric services to Earl's Court and the Metropolitan Railway ran an electric service, via Uxbridge Road, to Edgware Road.

For some time Addison Road was on the routes of both the Outer Circle, which operated from Broad

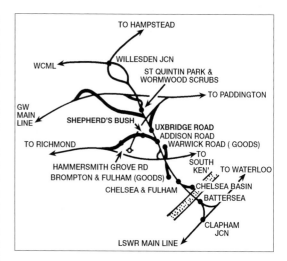

Street, via Willesden, to Mansion House, and the Middle Circle which ran from Moorgate, via Latimer Road also to Mansion House. Unlike the Inner Circle, these other circles were not particularly successful and services over the routes were eventually lost.

Below left: A Beattie 2-4-0WT of the LSWR stands at Addison Road station in 1872 with a train to Richmond, that would run via Shepherd's Bush and Hammersmith Grove Road. The locomotive was No 190, built in 1863.
Locomotive Publishing Co

Right: The disused LSWR line to Hammersmith swung away to the west at Addison Road station, where this view, taken in April 1998, shows one of the remaining bridges on the route. Having been abandoned in the 1930s most of the line has been built over, but a number of linear buildings clearly indicate the route of the old line. Author

Centre right: The remains of the former LSWR viaduct at Hammersmith, where the line from Addison Road once joined the District Line. Seen here in May 1997, an office comprehensively blocks the branch line in the distance. The tracks in the foreground are those of the District Line. Author

Below: A direction sign denoting access to Kensington Addison Road station and seen here in April 1998, over 40 years after the station was renamed Kensington Olympia. Author

Above: The Motorail terminal at Kensington Olympia. A seasonal service started from 1965 onwards and this view was taken shortly after opening. C. Gifford

Left: The disused Motorail terminal at Kensington Olympia, taken in April 1998. In 1975, car-carrying services from London ran to 15 locations in the UK. Services from this terminal ended in 1982. Author

Below left: The scale of facilities once provided for Motorail services at Kensington Olympia is apparent from this view taken in April 1998. The mass of cars parked on the site were connected with a nearby event being held at the Olympia exhibition halls. Author

In June 1916, all passenger services to Richmond over the line from Addison Road to Grove Road at Hammersmith were withdrawn. The main reason for closure was that more direct routes were available to Richmond from central London. Shepherd's Bush and Grove Road stations were closed, but the track was not removed from all sections of the line until the early 1930s and parts of the old viaduct that linked the branch to the District Line can still be seen at Hammersmith.

In 1917 the GWR opened a new connection to the north of Addison Road, at Viaduct Junction, to North Acton. However, passenger use declined on the remaining West London Line and services were gradually reduced. Nevertheless, it remained a key cross-London freight route. Consequently in October

1940, after the suspension of services because of severe bomb damage, it was decided to discontinue passenger services to all stations on the line.

After World War 2, a passenger revival came in December 1946 when Addison Road was renamed Kensington Olympia, and a shuttle service was reinstated to Earl's Court on exhibition days. Two morning and evening workmen's trains were also restored to Clapham Junction, but for a number of years these services were kept secret and were not advertised in public timetables. In 1967 these 'Kenny Belles', or 'Flyers' as they were also known, became the last local steam-hauled passenger services in London.

The passenger service from Clapham Junction to Kensington Olympia was identified in the Beeching Report for closure. Although this final cut was never implemented, the West London Line has seen many losses. The link to North Acton closed in March 1964. By 1966 Kensington Olympia was used for Motorail

services and new buildings were constructed, but these services were diverted to Euston in 1982 before Motorail services ceased operations altogether. All the freight depots along the line were also closed. Warwick Road depot closed in July 1967, milk traffic to Kensington ended in May 1972, West Brompton yard closed in August 1975 and sidings to the Thames, at Chelsea Basin, lasted until September 1981. A short link line to the GWR main line at North Pole closed in October 1990, in order to facilitate development of the Eurostar depot.

In 1987 a limited number of long-distance, north-south passenger services again used the route. Electrification has been reintroduced and regular passenger services now operate over the line. Although Kensington Olympia is currently the only intermediate station open, the platforms remain at Chelsea and there is much potential for station reopenings on the route.

Right: Map of railways in West London in 1938. Crown copyright

Above: An ex-SR Class W 2-6-4T, with a freight train, passes the Warwick Road freight depot in April 1955. The building in the far background, Charles House, was where the author worked for many years in an office with views onto the West London Line. G. Clarke

Below left: One of the last remains of the Kensington Canal, a lock-keeper's cottage located adjoining the site of the former Warwick Road goods yard, was being demolished to local uproar when this view was taken in August 1997. The West London Railway used the route of the old canal and originally had its boardroom in this area. Author

Above right: A Fairburn Tank, No 42101, based at Willesden shed, is seen here at West Brompton yard on 7 September 1962. The yard remained open until 1975. L. Sandler

Right: A Clapham Junction to Kensington van train passes the remaining buildings of Chelsea & Fulham station on 27 May 1950, hauled by Class M7 0-4-0T No 30038. This was one of the locomotives painted in malachite green at that time, to bring a splash of colour to the Clapham-Waterloo empty stock workings. E. Wethersett

18 Sheds, Steam and Smog

'Hell is a city much like London', remarked Shelley. The age of steam allowed London to grow and it became one of Britain's greatest manufacturing centres. The growth was accompanied by massive pollution and the atmosphere was not helped by the many hundreds of locomotives that at one time belched their steam and sometimes sulphurous smoke into the city's air. Fog, intensified by smoke, became the infamous 'pea soup' London smog. When this became particularly severe, special fog services were operated by the railways.

Being at the hub of the railway network there were a considerable number of locomotive sheds in the London area. They were of two main types, the roundhouse and the long shed. There had been a number of earlier shed closures, but in 1958 an extensive programme to eliminate steam traction was launched by BR and a decade later all the main line steam sheds in London had closed.

The former Eastern Region 'Top Shed', as King's Cross shed was known, contained an impressive array of locomotives used on the East Coast main line. In 1959 about 100 locomotives were to be found here and included famous names such as *Mallard* and *Flying Scotsman*, before closure came in June 1963.

Stratford was the largest shed in the country and in 1950 over 380 locomotives were to be found here. These were largely used on the world's most intensive steam suburban service that operated out of Liverpool Street before electrification. Although the steam shed closed in 1962, parts of the area are still in some form of railway use. Other ER sheds in the London area were to be found at Hornsey, Enfield and Walthamstow, and, from 1949, at Plaistow and Tilbury.

On the former Western Region, Old Oak Common was the largest ex-GWR steam shed and could house over 100 locomotives. Although the shed has been demolished and the site closed to steam in 1965, the general area remains in railway use. Southall shed was rebuilt in 1954, but closed in 1965. The shed was not demolished and is still used by preserved steam locomotives. Nearby Slough shed closed in 1964.

On the former London Midland Region, Camden was the leading passenger shed for the West Coast main line before its closure in 1962. The nearby Roundhouse, constructed in 1846 to designs by George Stephenson, is a notable exception to the mass of engine-shed demolitions in London. Willesden shed, classified as 1A, was the main London freight shed for the West Coast main line. In 1959 about 130 engines could be found here. Closure came in 1965.

The foremost passenger shed for the Midland main line was at Kentish Town and in 1959 about 100 engines could still be found here. Closure came in 1963. The main freight shed was at Cricklewood. By 1959 the allocation here had been reduced to about 50 locomotives and the shed closed in 1964. Other LMR sheds in the London area included Devons Row, which

---

Below: A notice warning passengers of the consequences of fog. The London smog was so thick on occasions that it delayed all movements of stock, created general operating difficulties and resulted in a revised timetable.
Author's collection

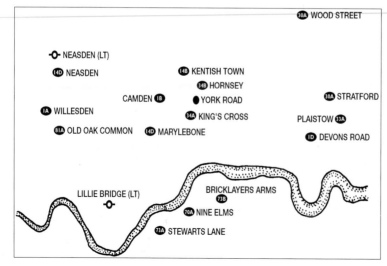

Right: Class A4 Gresley streamlined Pacific No 60026 Miles Beevor at King's Cross shed. Locomotives of this type were introduced in 1935 for working the 'Silver Jubilee', the first streamlined train to run out of London. The view here is taken towards the end of the locomotive's life; scrapping began in 1963, but a few remain in preservation.
Eric Treacy

Below: Diesels awaiting their turn of duty at King's Cross. Deltic, Brush Type 4, EE Type 4 and 'Peak' classes were all in evidence when this view was taken in the mid-1960s. St Pancras station looms in the background. Eric Treacy

was the former North London Railway shed at Bow. It was used by diesels prior to its closure in 1964. Neasden, which was taken over by the LMR in 1958, had a mixture of locomotives, including those from the former GCR. Sheds were also once to be found at Rickmansworth, Marylebone, Chesham and Watford.

Because of widespread electrification there were generally fewer sheds on the former Southern Region. The steam shed at Nine Elms dated back to the early days of the LSWR. At its peak about 200 engines were allocated here, but by 1965 this number was down to under 40. Nine Elms, which was essentially two adjoining sheds, suffered serious damage in World War 2, but was the last main line steam shed to close in London, lasting until July 1967. The area now has been completely redeveloped.

Other sheds on the Southern included Bricklayers Arms, where about 140 locomotives were to be found in 1950. This shed, which was also badly damaged in World War 2, was closed in 1962. Stewarts Lane was closed to steam in 1963. The concrete Feltham steam shed lasted until 1967, whilst that at Hither Green was one of the first to close in 1961.

On London Transport, smaller sheds could be found at Neasden on the Metropolitan Line, and Lillie Bridge on the District Line. Main line steam ended in London in 1967, but the final day of steam operation in London was on 6 June 1971 when one of London Transport's last three 0-6-0 pannier tanks ran into Neasden shed. Steam has gone from London, but on hot, still summer days the infamous smog returns.

Above: The 70ft-high reinforced concrete locomotive coaling plant being demolished by an explosive charge at King's Cross 'Top Shed' on 23 April 1964. Constructed in 1931 to hold 500 tons of coal and weighing 1,400 tons, this tower was not needed once the change to diesel had been made. British Railways

Below: GWR '47xx' class 2-8-0 at Old Oak Common shed. The huge steam shed, which consisted of four enclosed roundhouses, was designed by Churchward and opened in 1906. It was demolished in 1964, but the steam depot itself lingered on until the following year. C. R. L. Coles

Right: Map of Old Oak Common shed in 1938. Crown copyright

Centre right: GWR '57xx' class 0-6-0 pannier tank No 9706 with condensing apparatus. This equipment was unique to London engines that were used on the former Metropolitan Railway's Widened Lines to the Smithfield Market depot prior to its closure in 1962. The locomotive is seen here at Old Oak Common in March 1963. P. Williams

Below: A view of Camden shed in the 1950s, with a variety of steam engines polluting the air and seen here from the leading coach of the double-headed 8.50am Euston to Wolverhampton express. M. Welch

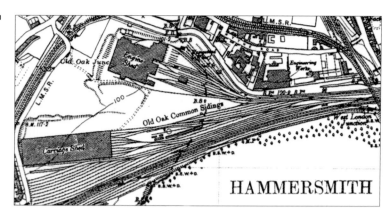

HAMMERSMITH

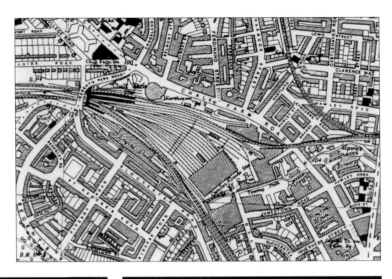

Above left: The original Roundhouse at Chalk Farm, viewed here in September 1997. The London & Birmingham Railway roundhouse was mainly designed by Robert Stephenson. The building, dating from 1847, soon became too small for the ever larger locomotives and was closed as far back as the 1860s. It was almost a century later that it was used as a theatre and is now to be turned into studios. Author

Above: Map of Camden shed and the Roundhouse in 1938. Crown copyright

Below: Ex-LMS Fowler Class 4 2-6-4T No 42334 at Kentish Town shed on 11 March 1962. The former Midland Railway passenger shed, which consisted of three enclosed roundhouses, was closed the following year. L. Sandler

Right: Ex-Somerset & Dorset Railway 'Jinty' Class 3F 0-6-0 No 47315, which was taken into LMS stock in 1936, seen here outside Devons Road shed on 8 October 1955. The shed was used by diesels from 1958 until its closure in 1964. B. Morrison

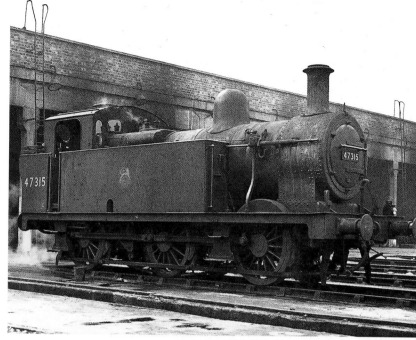

Below: Unrebuilt 'Battle of Britain' Pacific No 34066 Spitfire at Nine Elms shed, which was in fact two sheds side by side. This view is most likely to have been taken between 1957 and 1962, because of the clean condition of the locomotive. Scrapping of this class of locomotive commenced in 1963. Eric Treacy

Above: The run-down and almost derelict old shed at Nine Elms, just prior to the end of steam on the Southern Region in 1967. This area was one of the most heavily blitzed in London during World War 2, there were 92 incidents between Waterloo station and Queens Road station in 1940-1. K. Walker

Left: Bricklayers Arms shed on 19 March 1955. Class E6 0-6-2T No 3246 and Class H 0-4-4Ts Nos 31533, 31540 and 31542 are on shed. The area suffered much damage during World War 2. Real Photos

Right: London Transport's Neasden shed with pannier tanks L89 and L99 seen here in April 1969. The former steam shed remained in existence in 1998. V. Allen

Below: London Transport's Lillie Bridge shed with two pannier tanks seen from within the shed in 1968. At this time London Transport had nine steam engines in service at its Lillie Bridge and Neasden depots. The last regular steam train on LT and in London ran on 6 June 1971. K. Martin

The 6¼-mile single GWR line from West Drayton & Yiewsley station, to Staines looped off the earlier 2½-mile branch to Uxbridge Vine Street that opened in 1856. The Staines branch passed under the GWR main line, to reach Colnbrook in August 1884 and Staines by November 1885. At Staines an existing Georgian villa was converted into use as the terminus station.

The GWR Staines branch line did not have any major engineering works, but was forced to cross the LSWR Windsor branch to the north of Staines. Colnbrook was the main intermediate station, although it was actually located closer to Poyle. A number of halts were provided on the route. Runemede Range was opened in 1887 and renamed Yeoveney in 1935. A further halt was opened at Stanwell Moor & Poyle in 1927, although it was renamed Poyle in 1954. Colnbrook Estate Halt was opened in 1961.

During World War 2 there were concerns that lines in London would be blitzed out of action and alternative routes, avoiding central London, were examined to allow flexibility during air-raids. Consequently, a connection from the GWR to the Southern Railway was made at Staines in 1942, enabling the branch to operate as a through route for the first time.

After World War 2 the line continued to operate as a branch and soon after Nationalisation the GWR station was renamed Staines West. In July 1955 an hourly weekday service was provided between 7am and 10pm, with a not too dissimilar service on Sundays, trains taking 17min to cover the route with four stops. The timetable provided no details of connecting services to London; clearly the Southern route was to provide this service from Staines.

DMUs could not save the lines; services were withdrawn to Uxbridge Vine Street in 1962 and the Staines line was identified in the Beeching Report for closure. The last passenger services ran in March 1965. After this the branch was used for a while for experiments with Automatic Train Control. Freight continued to Uxbridge until 1964 and to the oil terminal, close to Staines West. In 1981 the line was cut by the new M25, but connection to the oil terminal at Staines was made from the former Southern line before the depot closed a decade later. A northern section of the former GWR branch remains open for freight as far as the Colnbrook industrial area. This

Right: Collett 0-4-2T No 1462 at Staines West shed on 25 June 1950. The locomotive was fitted with push-pull apparatus, for railmotor work on the branch. D. Sutton Collection

remaining section of single line was perhaps unique in having Junction 15 of the M25 built over it. The great investment in the motorway was in sharp contrast to the dilapidated fixed distant signal on the branch that could still be seen up to 1998.

Stations on the Uxbridge line have been demolished, but there are some interesting remains on the Staines branch, including the distinctive station house at Colnbrook, which denotes the current terminus of the freight route. The former automated level crossing now leads into a sea of brambles and a little further south the line has been truncated by the M25. At Staines West the distinctive and imposing listed terminus is in use as an office. Three of the original platform canopy supports have been retained in the car park. The

disused sidings to the nearby oil terminal also linger on. The original bridge over the former Southern line has been removed, but the World War 2 connection between the two lines is still apparent. Unlike the Uxbridge line, which has been mainly built over, part of the route to the north of Staines is in use as a footpath and bridleway. However, the wider potential of the line, first recognised during World War 2, is again being considered as part of studies looking at improved south and west rail links to Heathrow Airport.

Plans to link Uxbridge Vine Street with the GWR Denham to Uxbridge High Street line came to nothing and High Street station closed in August 1939, although coal traffic ran until 1962. A small part of the coalyard still remained in 1988.

Above: Locomotive-hauled stock at Uxbridge Vine Street. The branch to Staines West used a short section of the Uxbridge branch at West Drayton. The branch to Uxbridge Vine Street closed to passengers in 1962 and to all traffic two years later. Bob Barnard

Right: 0-4-2T No 1443 climbing from Yeoveney Halt with a train for Staines West on 24 April 1951. The halt was originally called Runemede Range, but its location some distance from Runnymede (note the different spelling) caused confusion and it was renamed Yeoveney Halt from November 1935. The halt closed in May 1962. The clean-cut embankment in this view has since become considerably overgrown.
D. Sutton Collection

Left: An 0-4-2T No1443 climbing from Yeoveney Halt with a train for Staines West on 24 April 1951. The halt closed in May 1962. The clean-cut embankment in this view has since become considererably overgrown. D. Sutton Collection

Below: A Staines West to West Drayton single railcar passing pannier tank No 4697 on the daily goods at Colnbrook on 8 June 1964. The GWR 0-6-0 pannier tank design numbered 863 in total and was once the most numerous of any class of locomotive in the country. T. Wright

Right: Branch railcar W55029 passing the 6.38am from Paddington, a through train to Staines West, at Colnbrook on 15 April 1964. T. Wright

Below right: The distinctive architecture of the station house at Colnbrook, which dates from 1884, is seen here in September 1997. The level crossing is no longer used, but freight trains continue to use the northern section of the branch as far as Colnbrook. Author

Table 51 — WEST DRAYTON & YIEWSLEY and STAINES WEST
(Third class only)

Week Days

Miles		am	am	am	am		am	am		E pm	S pm	pm	pm	pm	pm	pm	pm	E pm	pm	S pm	pm	pm	pm	pm
	West Drayton																							
	and Yiewsley .. dep	7 17	7 37	8 8	9 18	..	1012	1112	..	1212	1215	1 12	2 12	3 12	4 20	5 22	5 40	6 13	6 13	7 12	8 12	9 12	1012
3	Colnbrook	7 25	7C49	8 17	9 26	....	1020	1120	....	1220	1223	1 20	2 20	3 20	4F30	5 30	5C54	6J24	6 22	7 20	8 20	9 20	1020
—	Poyle Estate Halt ..[Halt	7 27	7 53	8 19	Rr	..	Rr	Rr	..	Rr	Rr	Rr	Rr	Rr	Rr	5 32	5 56	Rr	Rr	Rr	Rr	Rr	Rr
3½	Poyle, for Stanwell Moor,	7 29	7 55	8 21	9 30	....	1024	1124	....	1224	1227	1 24	2 24	3 24	4 35	5 58	6 26	7 24	8 24	9 24	1024
5½	Yeoveney	Rr	Rr	Rr	Rr	..	Rr	Rr	..	Rr	Rr	Rr	Rr	Rr	Rr	Rr	Rr	Rr	Rr	Rr	Rr	Rr	Rr
6½	Staines West ...... arr	7 34	8 1	8 27	9 35	....	1029	1129	....	1229	1233	1 29	2 29	3 29	4 41	5 39	6 4	6 33	6 31	7 29	8 29	9 29	1029

Sundays

		am		am		am	am		pm	pm	pm	pm		pm	pm		pm	pm		pm		pm	pm
	West Drayton																						
	and Yiewsley .. dep	7 9	..	9 9	..	10 9	11 9	..	12 9	1 9	2 9	3 9	....	4 9	5 9	..	6 9	7 9	..	8 9	..	9 9	10 9
	Colnbrook	7 17	....	9 17	....	1017	1117	..	1217	1 17	2 17	3 17	....	4 17	5 17	....	6 17	7 17	....	8 17	....	9 17	1017
	Poyle Estate Halt ..[Halt	Rr	..	Rr	..	Rr	Rr	..	Rr	Rr	Rr	Rr	....	Rr	Rr	..	Rr	Rr	..	Rr	..	Rr	Rr
	Poyle, for Stanwell Moor,	7 21	..	9 21	....	1021	1121	....	1221	1 21	2 21	3 21	..	4 21	5 21	....	6 21	7 21	....	8 21	....	9 21	1021
	Yeoveney	Rr	..	Rr	..	Rr	Rr	..	Rr	Rr	Rr	Rr	..	Rr	Rr	..	Rr	Rr	..	Rr	..	Rr	Rr
	Staines West ...... arr	7 26	....	9 26	....	1026	1126	....	1226	1 26	2 26	3 26	..	4 26	5 26	....	6 26	7 26	....	8 26	....	9 26	1026

Week Days

Miles		am	am	am	am		am	am	am		pm	pm	pm	pm	pm	pm		E pm	pm	pm	pm	pm	pm
—	**Staines West ..** .. dep	6 44	7 37	8 5	8 38	..	9 40	1040	1140	..	1240	1 40	2 40	3 40	4 54	5 42	..	6 12	6 38	7 40	8 40	9 40	1040
1	Yeoveney...........[Halt	Rr	Rr	Rr	Rr	....	Rr	Rr	Rr	....	Rr	Rr	Rr	Rr	Rr	Rr	..	Rr	Rr	Rr	Rr	Rr	Rr
2½	Poyle, for Stanwell Moor,	6 49	7 42	8 10	8 43	..	9 45	1045	1145	..	1245	1 45	2 45	3 45	4 59	5 47	..	6 17	6 43	7 45	8 45	9 45	1045
—	Poyle Estate Halt	6 51	7 44	8 12	8 45	....	9 47	Rr	Rr	....	Rr	Rr	Rr	Rr	5 1	Rr	..	6 19	Rr	Rr	Rr	Rr	Rr
3½	Colnbrook	6 53	7 47	8L20	8 47	..	9 49	1049	1149	..	1249	1 49	2 49	3 49	5 4	5 52	..	6 21	6 47	7 49	8 49	9 49	1049
6½	**West Drayton**																						
	and Yiewsley .. arr	7 1	7 55	8 28	8 55	....	9 57	1057	1157	....	1257	1 57	2 57	3 57	5 12	6 0	....	6 29	6 56	7 57	8 57	9 57	1057

Sundays

		am		am		am		am		pm	pm	pm		pm	pm		pm	pm		pm	pm		pm	pm
	Staines West .. .. dep	8 7	..	9 37	..	1037	..	1137	..	1237	1 37	2 37	..	3 37	4 37	..	5 37	6 37	..	7 37	8 37	..	9 37	1037
	Yeoveney..........[Halt	Rr	....	Rr	....	Rr	....	Rr	....	Rr	Rr	Rr	....	Rr	Rr	....	Rr	Rr	....	Rr	Rr	....	Rr	Rr
	Poyle, for Stanwell Moor,	8 12	..	9 42	..	1042	..	1142	..	1242	1 42	2 42	..	3 42	4 42	..	5 42	6 42	..	7 42	8 42	..	9 42	1042
	Poyle Estate Halt	Rr	....	Rr	....	Rr	....	Rr	....	Rr	Rr	Rr	....	Rr	Rr	....	Rr	Rr	....	Rr	Rr	....	Rr	Rr
	Colnbrook	8 16	..	9 46	....	1046	..	1146	..	1246	1 46	2 46	..	3 46	4 46	..	5 46	6 46	..	7 46	8 46	..	9 46	1046
	West Drayton																								
	and Yiewsley ... arr	8 24	....	9 54	....	1054	....	1154	....	1254	1 54	2 54	....	3 54	4 54	....	5 54	6 54	....	7 54	8 54	....	9 54	1054

C Arrive 7 45 am
E Except Saturdays
F Arrive 4 28 pm
G Arrive 5 48 pm
J Arrive 6 21 pm
L Arrive 8 14 am

Rr Calls to set down and take up passengers. Those wishing to alight must inform the Guard at West Drayton or Staines West, and passengers desiring to join should give the necessary hand signal to the driver. Trains dep Poyle Estate Halt 2 minutes after leaving Colnbrook or Poyle, for Stanwell Moor Halt. Trains dep from Yeoveney 2 minutes after leaving Poyle for Stanwell Moor Halt or Staines West
S Saturdays only

Above: The Staines West branch timetable in July 1955. Author's collection

Right: The white bricks of Staines West station bathed in autumn sunshine when this view was taken in September 1997. The substantial former dwelling was converted into a station by the GWR when the railway arrived in the town. Currently in use as offices, the rear car park contains some of the original iron supporting columns from the platform canopy. Author

Above: A view of tracks that once served the oil depot at Staines West. This depot opened in 1964 and was served by the branch until the M25 severed the line to the north of Staines in 1981. After this, the terminal was accessed from the nearby Southern Region line. The terminal was last used in 1991, but tracks still remained at Staines West when this view was taken, in September 1997. Author

Above: Part of the line has been turned into a footpath to the north of Staines, as can be seen in this view taken in September 1997. Plans for greater rail access to Heathrow Airport could possibly see the reuse of part of this branch. Author

20 Sunday at Stanmore

There were once two lines to Stanmore; one still remains (now on the Jubilee Line), but the original railway has long since closed. The Harrow & Stanmore Railway, soon to become part of the LNWR, opened in December 1890. It ran from Harrow & Wealdstone station some two miles in a northeasterly direction to Stanmore. The line was promoted by a businessman who owned the nearby Bentley Priory Hotel and saw the railway as a useful way of bringing custom from London to these country areas.

There was opposition to the railway and concerns over the station at Stanmore led to a design that was most distinctive — the station's own spire competing with the local church. It was also agreed that there should be no trains on Sundays for some considerable time. At the other end of the line the junction station at Harrow & Wealdstone was reconstructed in 1901, to the design of Gerald Horsley, with a handsome clock tower.

A halt was provided at Belmont in September 1932. This area was experiencing considerable growth and the small wooden shelter and flimsy buildings, which were originally located in green fields, were replaced

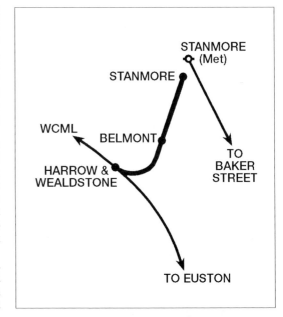

Left: An Ivatt 2-6-2T, No 41220, stands at Stanmore Village with a two-coach train for Harrow & Wealdstone station in July 1952. Few passengers are to be seen and the line closed two months later. Ian Allan Library

Above: Although Stanmore closed to passengers in 1952, a special train visited the remaining freight-only section from Belmont on a Railway Correspondence & Travel Society Hertfordshire Rail Tour, on 27 April 1958. The train is seen here at Stanmore Village, shortly before departure, behind Stanier 0-4-4T No 41901. David Lawrence

by more permanent and larger structures in 1937. A relatively frequent weekday service developed, although the line remained single.

The LMS station at Stanmore was located on the southwestern fringe of the settlement. The alternative Metropolitan Railway's electrified route, with a frequent service to London, opened in December 1932. The new electrified line enabled passengers from Stanmore to reach central London without the need for a change of trains. This made the section from Belmont to Stanmore Village an early candidate for closure and passenger services ceased in September 1952, although freight continued.

In October 1952, early morning commuters from Belmont were to witness at Harrow & Wealdstone station London's worst railway accident. A train from Tring, that provided connections to London from the branch, was on that day using the fast line as the preceding express from Perth was running late. As the Tring train waited at Harrow the express from Perth smashed into its rear. Almost immediately from the other direction a double-headed express from Euston collided into the wreckage of the first crash — 112 persons were killed.

Services to Belmont continued and experimental diesel railcars were operated over this short section of branch in 1954. After a brief return to steam haulage, standard DMUs were introduced in 1957. Considerable commuting developed from Belmont. In 1955 the 1¼-mile trip took 3min and up to six trains an hour were provided to Harrow & Wealdstone station on weekdays. However, the Beeching Report identified the route for closure. Over 1,000 petitioned against this, but to no avail. The line, including the remaining freight service to Stanmore, closed in October 1964. The route was used for filming purposes in 1965-6, after which it was abandoned.

Small parts of the original station at Stanmore have been incorporated into a new house and the station yard has been turned into a residential area. At Belmont the track can still be traced and part is used as a footway. At Harrow & Wealdstone the branch platform remains hardly unchanged since the last branch train pulled out, although the track has been removed.

Above: The distinctive design of Stanmore station as seen from the road. The station was completed in 1890, renamed Stanmore Village in 1950, closed in 1952 and subsequently demolished. David Lawrence

Below left: Although the original station at Stanmore was demolished, a new house on the station site incorporated some aspects of the earlier building into its construction. The unique stone window from the original station is seen here in September 1997. Author's collection

Above right: An experimental ACV diesel set at Belmont on 21 March 1959. Belmont was opened in 1932 as the only intermediate station on the branch. The area saw considerable growth and for many years it was highly successful. From 1952 Belmont functioned as the passenger terminus of the line before it was also closed in 1964. G. Kichenside

Right : The former trackbed at Belmont in September 1997, used as part of the Belmont Nature Walk run by the London Wildlife Trust. The former line here is in an urban area, but has become heavily overgrown, providing an attractive green linear corridor. Author

Far right: The disused branch platform for Stanmore still remained at Harrow & Wealdstone station when this view was taken in October 1997. A plaque in memory of the 112 people killed in the train crash at Harrow & Wealdstone was unveiled near the station in 1997, some 45 years after the accident. Author

Below right: The intensive Harrow & Wealdstone and Belmont timetable in 1955. Author's collection

Table 59	HARROW and WEALDSTONE and BELMONT—(Third Class only)

Week Days only

Where MINUTES under Hours change to a LOWER figure and DARKER type it indicates NEXT HOUR

E Except Saturdays   S Saturdays only

21 West of Watford

Watford is unique for the number of stations that serve the town. These include Junction, High Street, North, West, Stadium and just plain Watford. The main station is Watford Junction and from here two routes once ran westward.

Lord Ebury was granted powers to construct a line from Watford to Rickmansworth and in October 1862 a 4½-mile route opened between the two towns. The terminus at Rickmansworth was located almost opposite the church to the south of the town and interchange sidings were provided with the nearby Grand Union Canal. The line, which had no intermediate stations after Watford High Street, was never particularly successful and only four years after opening the Official Receiver was called in.

In 1881 the line became part of the LNWR, which became increasingly concerned about the growing influence of the Metropolitan Railway in this part of northwest London. As a consequence a second short line was added to Croxley Green. Work on this branch was started in 1908 and the new route opened in June 1912. The terminus at Croxley Green, in its semi-rural

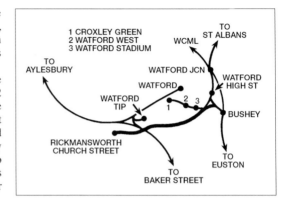

Below: An ex-LNWR Oerlikon electric unit is seen at Rickmansworth Church Street station on 25 August 1951. At this time Church Street had been added to the station's name, to distinguish it from the Metropolitan Line station. The station closed to passengers in March 1952. M. Casserley

location, added credence to the LNWR's slogan 'Live in the Country'. The route involved a substantial bridge over the Grand Union Canal, but the line was to end just beyond at the small terminus at Croxley Green. In March 1913 the station at Croxley Green was burned down by suffragettes. The replacement station for many years stood gauntly on its embankment, until the building was demolished by British Railways.

Electric services were introduced to Croxley Green in October 1922 and to Rickmansworth in September 1927. A few trains ran directly from Croxley Green to both Euston and Broad Street. However, electric services, including some through services to London, were not to save the Rickmansworth line which suffered strong competition from the more direct services to London on the Metropolitan Railway.

Left: Much of the old trackbed from Watford to Rickmansworth is used as a footpath and a number of remains of the line are still visible on the route, as this view of a small bridge taken in September 1997 shows. Author

Below: A Locomotive Club of Great Britain special has arrived on the overgrown tracks at Rickmansworth Church Street station. The electric conductor rails have gone and final closure of this section of the branch to remaining freight services came in 1966. David Lawrence

After Nationalisation, Church Street was added to the station's name to distinguish it from that on the Metropolitan Line, but passenger services to Rickmansworth were withdrawn in March 1952. Regular freight services ceased in 1966, although some freight remained to the Goodyear Tyre siding on the line for a time after this. After closure the station buildings at Rickmansworth were used for business purposes, before demolition and redevelopment of the site. A very considerable length of the trackbed of the former Rickmansworth branch is used as a footpath known as the Ebury Way.

Although identified in the Beeching Report for closure, consent to shut the line to Croxley Green was refused. A peak hour service was run for many years and in the end this was reduced to one train a day in each direction. Then a new road cut the route between Watford West and Croxley Green and services were replaced by a bus. Elsewhere, the track and stations remain and a new connection from the Watford branch of the Metropolitan Line to the Croxley branch is in prospect.

Above: Although closure of the Croxley Green branch was refused, services were cut back. The last rush hour train of the morning, the 09.12, is seen departing from Croxley Green for Watford Junction on 1 December 1971. The eventual service of one train a day in each direction was suspended and a bus service was substituted, but there are plans to reopen the line. G. Cocks

Finally, at the south end of the triangular junction that provides access to the Metropolitan branch to Watford, London Transport once had a waste tip which was served by freight trains from Neasden depot. Watford Tip closed about 1970 and has since become overgrown, but remains of the track to the tip could still be seen in the undergrowth in 1998.

Above:
The substantial bridge over the Grand Union Canal just beyond Croxley Green station, seen here in September 1997. However, a short way beyond this bridge the line has currently been severed by a new road. Author

Right: Watford West station on the electrified route to Croxley Green. The station buildings have been demolished and the mothballed station is seen here in September 1997, with buffers beyond preventing use of the line towards Croxley Green. Author

Above: London Transport's rubbish train at Watford tip on 7 October 1969. Ex-GWR 0-6-0PT No L99 is seen here leaving the Watford line and travelling along the spur to the tip sidings. The side of the steam crane can just be seen in the left-hand foreground. The route of the old spur to the tip could still be traced here in 1998. G. Merrin

Below: Ex-GWR 0-6-0PT No L92 shunts at Watford tip on 19 August 1969. A train was timetabled to run daily, but at this time ran only on a Monday with any regularity. The tip has since been allowed to return to nature and today much of the area supports a small wood. H. McIntyre

22 Return to Ongar

In April 1865 the line from Epping to Ongar was opened by the GER. It formed part of a longer 11½-mile route that diverged away from the original terminus at Loughton and ran via Epping, over the attractive Rodings, to Ongar. Extensions to Great Dunmow and Bury St Edmunds were contemplated, together with the idea of creating a loop line to Chelmsford, but the remote area was hardly conducive to railway construction and Ongar was to remain the rural terminus.

At the other end of the line it was in fact congestion into Liverpool Street that led to a number of routes being transferred to the London Underground. In 1949 the branch to Ongar was to become part of the Central Line, with electric trains running to Epping by that year. Nevertheless, Ongar remained served by a steam shuttle until November 1957, after which electric tube trains started to run the shuttle.

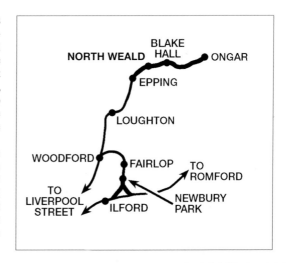

Right: A Class F5 2-4-2T, No 67200, is seen leaving Ongar with the 2.43pm push-pull service to Epping on 28 April 1956. Although at this time the line was part of London Transport, it retained a rural branch line atmosphere. P. Kelley

Above: Electric services between Epping and Ongar started in November 1957. In this view an Epping train is seen leaving Ongar on 28 April 1962 with cars Nos 3006, 7438 and 3008. L. Sandler

Left: LT 1959 underground stock arriving at Ongar from Epping on 28 May 1981. By this time the former GER signalbox had closed and a number of economy measures had been introduced, including speed restrictions. B. Morrison

Right: The Epping and Ongar timetable in July 1955.

The new 'tubes' always looked a little out of place as they rattled through the remote Essex countryside on this typically Great Eastern branch line. Indeed this may well have been one of the few routes on London Transport to boast of snow fences to prevent drifting onto exposed parts of the line. Although electrified, the Epping to Ongar scheme was done 'on the cheap' with power sufficient only to run either two four-car sets or one eight-car set on the line. As such the new services were always limited and involved a change of trains at Epping.

The introduction of electric services on the route saw passenger numbers increase and between 5am and midnight there were almost 40 weekday departures from Ongar. None the less, being at the extremity of the line, the relatively slow service (my diary for a 1970 trip on the line notes: 'slow is not the word'), the change required at Epping and, in later years, the relatively infrequent service all conspired to lead to decline. Blake Hall station, which served a remote rural area had the dubious distinction of being the least used station on the entire underground network. Calls were made for the closure of the branch in the 1970s. As it turned out the line was reprieved and economies were made, but the service worsened, becoming peak hour only. In October 1981 Blake Hall station was closed and eventually, after years of uncertainty, which did not help patronage, the line closed in September 1994.

This is not the end of the story. The track remains and the line is to be run by a private company. All the station buildings remain and Blake Hall's enamel nameboard is preserved at the London Transport Museum.

Associated with the line to Ongar is the Fairlop Loop. In May 1903, the 6¼-mile loop line was opened by the GER, linking Woodford to a triangular junction at Ilford, which gave access to both London and to Seven Kings in an area that was later to become part of the Ilford maintenance depot. In 1947 this loop also became a section of the Central Line and electric tube trains operated over the loop as far as a new station at Newbury Park. The remaining line, south to Ilford, was used for freight until complete closure in March 1956. Today, although all the bridges remain on this closed section, most of the cutting has been filled in and much of the area created is used as allotments.

Above: The abandoned station platform at Ongar in September 1997. Although designed as a through station, with the possibility of extensions to the line, Ongar was to remain the rural terminus of the branch. Author

Table 15a — EPPING and ONGAR—Third Class only

Week Days

All trains call at North Weald (2½ miles) and Blake Hall (4½ miles) 7 and 14 minutes respectively after leaving Epping

E Except Saturdays. H Runs 4 minutes *earlier* on Saturdays. J Runs 3 minutes later on Saturdays. K Runs 7 minutes *earlier* on Saturdays. L Runs 8 minutes later on Saturdays. N Runs 5 minutes later on Saturdays. P Runs 12 minutes later on Saturdays. S Saturdays only. V Runs 4 minutes later on Saturdays. Y Runs 8 minutes *earlier* on Saturdays Z Runs 14 minutes *earlier* on Saturdays

London Transport (Central Line) trains run at frequent intervals between Liverpool Street (Central Line) and Epping, calling at Bethnal Green 3, Mile End 6, Stratford 9, Leyton 12, Leytonstone 15, Snaresbrook 17, South Woodford 19, Woodford 22, Buckhurst Hill 25, Loughton 28, Debden 32, Theydon Bois 36 and Epping 40 minutes after leaving Liverpool Street.

Where MINUTES under Hours change to a LOWER figure and DARKER type it indicates NEXT HOUR

Left: An attempt is being made to reuse the Epping to Ongar line. This was not helped by the attentions of graffiti vandals to stock, seen here at Ongar in September 1997. Author

Below: The remote Blake Hall station. Of a typical GER design, dating from 1865, it is viewed here on 1 March 1977, with LT 1962 underground stock leaving for Epping. J. Glover

Above: The rural tube: an Ongar to Epping train about to run into Blake Hall station on 17 May 1980. Although in a rural area, at one time milk and other perishable goods would have been sent to London from the station. P. Groom

Right: Blake Hall had the distinction of eventually becoming the least used of all London Transport's stations. The station closed in November 1981 and the platforms had been removed when this view was taken in September 1997. Author

Above: North Weald station once provided a useful service to the nearby airfield. It is seen here in September 1997, awaiting the return of a train service. A single fare to Liverpool Street from this station in the 1930s cost 4s 2d (21p). Author

Left: One of the substantial bridges on the closed section of the Hainault loop line, to the south of Newbury Park. The bridge is viewed here in September 1997. Author

23 The London That Never Was

The station at Brill and the surrounding remote rural area is just over 50 miles from London and was as far removed from the roar of traffic and cosmopolitan grandeur of Baker Street station as you could get. Yet both stations were once part of the Metropolitan Railway and later London Transport.

At Quainton Road a light railway struck off westward on low-lying land towards Brill. The line, which followed the roadside for much of the first part of its route, opened to near Wotton in March 1871 and by March of the following year reached the foot of Brill Hill. The main purpose of the line, for a time, was to carry goods and construction material for Waddesdon Manor.

The branch, known as the Brill, or Wotton Tramway, was lightly constructed and for a while traffic was horse-drawn. However, from January 1872 it was worked by light Aveling & Porter locomotives and, by popular demand, also conveyed passengers. In 1888 the Oxford & Aylesbury Tramroad leased the tramway and proposed an extension to Oxford.

The Metropolitan Railway, which by 1891 ran trains out from Baker Street to Quainton Road and beyond to the equally remote Verney Junction, took over the tramway in December 1899. The line became known

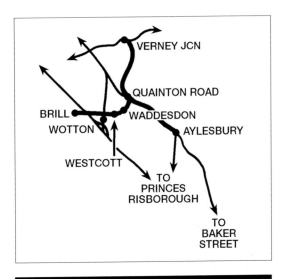

Below: Quainton Road station, with an arrival at the Brill Tramway platform of a one-coach train, hauled by 0-6-0ST Wotton No 2. The tramway was also known as the Wotton Tramway, or even the Hedgerow Tramway. Locomotive Publishing Co

as its Brill branch. On some Metropolitan route maps the branch was shown as a fork, on a par in importance with the main line to Aylesbury and that to Verney Junction.

The Met acted as both a transport concern and property speculator. The design of residential estates and even the houses was carried out by a subsidiary of the railway and the name 'Metroland' was coined in 1915. Wherever the railway went, green fields near stations were transformed into suburban areas. The Met primarily saw the Brill branch as a part of its future link to Oxford and the West Midlands. Nevertheless, there was a suspicion that this enterprising railway also had aspirations to extend Metroland into this peaceful backwater. Even if residential development was slow to come, Brill could always be promoted as a spa town.

However, any optimism of this area becoming part of London's suburbia was soon dispelled. The Met worked the line with a single coach and it generated

Above: Metropolitan 4-4-0T No 23, dating from 1866 and built by Beyer Peacock & Co, ambles along the branch during the short period when London Transport ran the line before closure in 1935. The locomotive, which was retired in 1948, can now be seen in the London Transport Museum, together with one of the Aveling & Porter locomotives that were also once used on the line. H. C. Casserley

Below: Wotton station is located behind the camera in this view taken in 1935, the last year of the branch. The Great Central, Ashendon Junction to Grendon Underwood line crosses over the bridge. Real Photos

little revenue. The proposals which would have utilised the route as an alternative link to Oxford came to nothing. In 1906 the branch became part of the Met & GCR Joint Committee, but it continued as a sleepy backwater until it reluctantly became part of the London Passenger Transport Board in 1933.

When London Transport took over it did not consider this remote rural branch to be part of its London network. The station at Brill was scarcely convenient for the hilltop settlement and alternative main line stations were to be found at Wotton and Brill & Ludgershall. The fastest train took about two hours to reach London and what traffic there was had fallen away. The line was closed in November 1935.

The last day saw hundreds turn out in the rain to say goodbye to this branch of great character and charm. The assets were later sold off and as the line was lightly constructed, parts are no longer distinguishable in the landscape. Yet much of interest remains. At Quainton Road the Brill platform and waiting room are preserved as part of the Buckinghamshire Railway Centre. The first section of tramway, from Quainton Road to Waddesdon Road and Westcott, is used as a footpath and the station cottages at Wotton and Westcott, dated 1871, remain. The bridge under the Great Central line at Wotton is no more, together with the bridge over the ex-GWR line near Brill, although the abutments and fencing of the latter are still visible.

Two locomotives that once used the line have been preserved. One of the original lightweight locomotives, built by Aveling & Porter at Rochester in 1872 and essentially a traction engine on railway wheels, was located in a brickworks after the line closed. It is now preserved at London Transport's Museum in London, together with 'A' class 4-4-0T Met Tank No 23, dating from 1866, that was also once used on the line.

The Met's line to Verney Junction closed in July 1936 and is covered in the *Lost Lines: LMR* volume. The rural leg of the Met, from Aylesbury to Amersham, reverted from London Transport to British Railways in 1961, perhaps finally ending the Met's aspirations to expand London into this area.

Above: A similar situation at Wotton in September 1997. The GCR overbridge has been removed after closure in 1966, but the route of the tramway can still be clearly traced at this location. Author

Left: The line once crossed the former GWR & GCR Joint Line, now the Chiltern Line, east of Brill, at this point. The bridge had long since been removed when this view was taken in September 1997. More encouragingly, the remaining railway line seen here is experiencing increased traffic. Author

Right: The Brill branch after the track had been upgraded through woodland between Wotton and Wood Siding. The rural character of this extremity of the Metropolitan Railway is evident from this view. Ian Allan Library

Below: A fascinating view of Wood Siding station. A country idyll, yet under detailed scrutiny the photograph reveals more than just a man with a flag. Timetables for the Metropolitan and Great Central Railways are supplemented by posters concerning military service, one with the famous 'Your country needs you' slogan. Two guns and kit-bags lean on the shed, all indicating that this view dates from World War 1. Ian Allan Library

Above: Wood Siding in London Transport days, with Metropolitan 4-4-0T No 23 and a single coach departing the station. The attractive view is framed by the loading gauge, an essential item of equipment that prevented wagons being loaded over a specified height. Real Photos

Below: Metropolitan Railway Class H 4-4-4T, built by Kerr Stuart in 1920-1 and seen here waiting at Verney Junction on 2 May 1936. Passenger services over the former Metropolitan Railway's branch to this station ended shortly after, in July 1936. Today the platforms are still visible and a single mothballed line, part of the former Oxford to Cambridge route, passes through the site. Plans to reopen this mothballed route are under consideration, but the likelihood of reopening Verney Junction is currently as remote as its location. H. Casserley

The London & Croydon, London & Greenwich and the London & Blackwall railways were all early examples of lines in London with relatively closely-spaced stations and frequent trains that were built specifically for the commuter. The Blackwall line ceased to carry commuters in 1926, but the problem with most lines in London was providing for peak hour capacity.

The difficulty of supplying sufficient seats for peak-hour London commuters, within the confines of the British main line loading gauge, led to the use of a bench seat across the entire width of the carriage. The Great Eastern widened older carriages to provide for six 3rd class seats and in later years Bulleid designed curved-sided coaches on the Southern in an attempt to create a little more width for the six seats.

The single compartments had the advantage that they could seat 12, but their lack of communication with the rest of the train led to problems of vandalism, sex and violence. Franz Müller killed Thomas Briggs in an enclosed compartment on the North London Railway in 1864, but the use of such compartments lingered on for London's commuters right into the early 1990s. For 20 years I was one such commuter, travelling for a decade on the Eastern Region and for a similar period on the Southern Region, very often in non-corridor compartments. A notice above the benches indicated 'six seats', but I can confirm that the comfort level ended after the fifth commuter was seated. On almost all journeys nothing untoward happened, but travelling every day, over many years, a number of incidents were inevitably recorded in my diary.

Just as the design of suburban coaches had not changed much over the years, nor had unsocial behaviour. The single compartments continued to be the scenes of some ugly incidents. On arrival at Victoria one morning a train from Orpington was cordoned off after staff found a murdered woman in one of the single compartments. After this incident a distinctive identifying warning stripe was applied to the outside of non-corridor compartments.

The enclosed compartments were a temptation for all sorts of other activity. They were a real trap: you just had to wait until the next station stop if someone smelt unpleasant, was drunk, or acted in a disagreeable way. Passengers rarely spoke, except to complain. One evening two lads entered a non-smoking compartment and asked if anyone minded if they smoked. I suspect everyone did mind, but no one had the courage to say so. Out came 'reefers' as their 'trip' sped on. Brazen behaviour could also occasionally occur on such trains.

Below: As passenger numbers increased, the capacity of routes to handle the growth in traffic became a problem. The most intensive steam commuter service in the world was operated out of Liverpool Street station; even the coaches were cut in half and widened to provide extra seats. The GER first-class coach, illustrated here by Mr Ventura, is preserved at the East Anglian Railway Centre. Author's collection

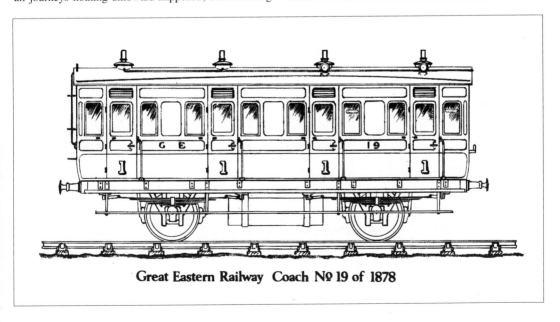

Great Eastern Railway Coach Nº 19 of 1878

Travelling over the Ilford flyover, late one night, I could not help but notice a couple making love on a bench seat in a carriage travelling below.

On Müller's train there was no communication cord. They were introduced as a result of such murders mentioned above and for other emergencies. On one occasion my train from Liverpool Street failed to stop, as advertised, at Brentwood, so someone pulled the communication cord. The train screeched to a halt outside the station. An angry driver walked along the track remonstrating that this was an improper use of the cord. When we eventually arrived at the next station, Shenfield, all those for Brentwood were ushered into an office and the driver asked who had shouted abuse at him. A big passenger came forward and with further obscenities made it clear that it was him. Things were looking ugly, but then a train back to Brentwood was announced, everyone rushed out of the office and jumped on the returning train. All arrived home late, but with a great yarn to tell.

There were also other incidents, but they were not the norm. Of course, some trains will inevitably be delayed or cancelled and some of London's commuters will no doubt have their own understanding of Robert Louis Stevenson's words: 'To travel hopefully is a better thing than to arrive', but, in general, the enormous number of trains that run each day within and to and from London are a testament to a truly magnificent and civilised form of travel. London's very existence, as we know it today, is to a large extent due to the influence of the railways. Its future prosperity and role as a world city will continue to be inexorably linked to its railways.

Above left: Bulleid's distinctive door design on a commuter carriage that had been widened as far as possible to provide maximum seating capacity. In this view, an off-peak commuter train speeds the author and his thoughts to his home in 1990. Author

Left: The quietest platform on London's busiest station. The northerly Platform 1 at Clapham Junction, awaiting passengers from Chelsea, Battersea and other lost London destinations, viewed here in April 1998. Author